SOM
RAN

SOMERSET RAMBLES
Fourteen Country Walks around Somerset

Nigel Vile

————

With Historical Notes

COUNTRYSIDE BOOKS
NEWBURY, BERKSHIRE

COUNTRYSIDE BOOKS
3 Catherine Road
Newbury, Berkshire
ISBN 1 85306 034 8

Cover photograph of the Quantocks
taken by Matthew Stevens

Produced through MRM Associates, Reading
Typeset by Acorn Bookwork, Salisbury
Printed in England by J. W. Arrowsmith Ltd., Bristol

To my wife Gill and children Laura, Katie and James

Acknowledgement

I would like to thank Brian Martyn who gave me much valuable help and advice in the preparation of this book.

Contents

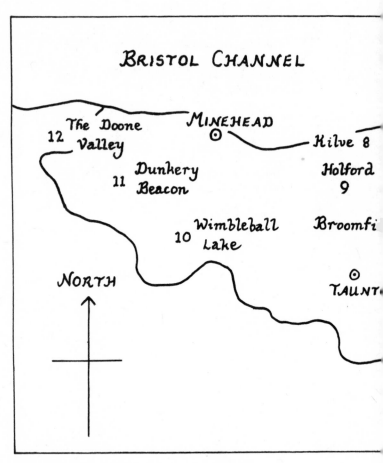

Sketch map showing locations of walks

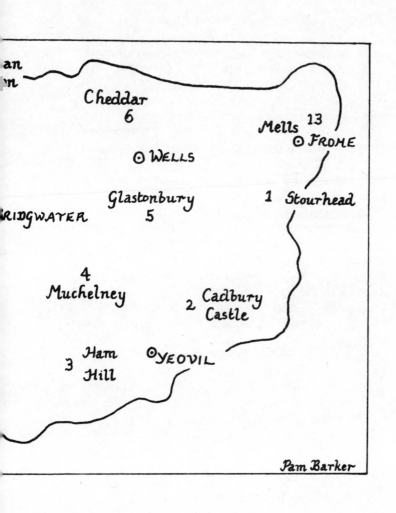

an
'n

Cheddar
6

Mells 13
⊙ FROME

⊙ WELLS

Glastonbury
5

1 Stourhead

RIDGWATER

4
Muchelney

2 Cadbury
Castle

3 Ham
Hill

⊙ YEOVIL

Pam Barker

Introduction

Winding lanes and overgrown hedgerows, cider and cheese, cream teas in cottage gardens, and the sound of leather-on-willow echoing across a thousand village greens – this is the very essence of Somerset. For the rambler the county is virtually unbeatable for the sheer variety of its landscape – craggy uplands or open moorlands, flat wetlands or clifftop paths, forest tracks or fortified hilltops.

The derivation of the county name provides an interesting insight into its history: 'Seo-mere-seatan' – 'dwellers by the sealakes' refers to the early settlers at the lake villages of Glastonbury and Meare, whose homes were simple wooden huts sited on grassy mounds above the marshes, now known as the 'Somerset Levels'. To the north of the Levels rises the massive limestone upland of the Mendips with its intriguing network of caves and pot-holes, dry river valleys and gorges. To the east, along the Wiltshire border stretch the remnants of the ancient Selwood Forest, a natural divide between Wessex and the West Country.

In south Somerset the hills are perhaps more isolated but of much greater prominence due to their isolation. To the west the landscape becomes dominated by upland regions of considerable repute – the Quantocks, the Brendons and, of course, the Exmoor National Park. The Somerset coast offers a mixture of rocky headlands and mud-flats, miniature cliffs and sandy shores.

The greatest difficulty in compiling this book has undoubtedly been narrowing the choice down to just 14 locations. I hope that this selection will give the visitor and resident alike a taste of the many types of landscape that Somerset can offer, each ramble offering as fine an example as it has been possible to find.

Each of the 14 circular rambles comes complete with details of parking and refreshment arrangements, together with approximate estimates of the distance and timing for the circuit. A personal selection of historical notes has also been included to enable the landscapes and landmarks, the villages and the people to be placed into some sort of historical context.

Each ramble was planned using the Ordnance Survey 1:25 000 series of maps, that show clearly the public rights-of-way, although occasionally it may be necessary to let common sense prevail, especially where arable farming predominates. For those who like to use 1:50 000 series the sheets which cover the county are 180, 181, 182, 183 and 193. The grid reference relates to the starting point.

Several of the rambles do take us onto high upland regions where cloud can quickly descend to completely envelop the landscape. In such an environment, it should go without saying that stout footwear and waterproofs are a must.

Finally, may I wish you every pleasure in walking these delightful footpaths and bridleways.

Nigel Vile
March 1989

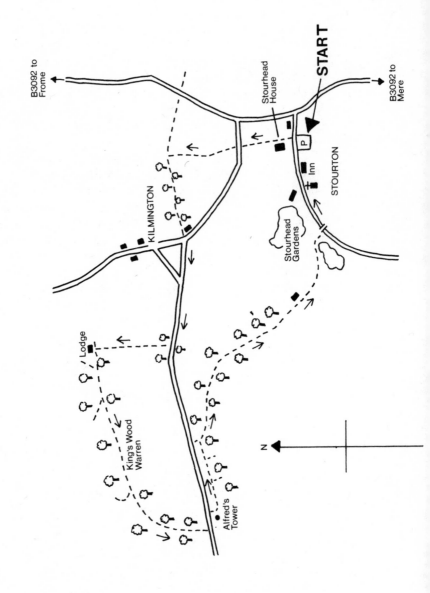

Stourhead and the Wiltshire border

Introduction: Stourhead, with its world-famous landscaped gardens and interesting house, provides the perfect starting point for this border ramble. The walk leaves the splendours of Stourhead to climb to Alfred's Tower from the top of which fine views can be gained. Opening hours are restricted and should be checked in advance (see Historical Notes). The walk passes through remnants of the ancient Selwood Forest which forms a natural divide between Wessex and the West Country. SPB Mais, writing in 1938 in *Walking in Somerset*, thought this the very best way to enter Somerset, descending from Alfred's Tower to 'a gentle smiling land of little rivers, orchards, dairy farms and hamlets nestling among trees on the sides of a score of curiously irregular knolls'.

Distance: This ramble covers a good 6 miles. 3 hours should be sufficient time to complete the circuit comfortably.

Refreshments: In the village of Stourton, where the walk starts and finishes, there is the National Trust's *Spread Eagle Inn*. As well as liquid refreshment, the *Spread Eagle* offers lunches, bar snacks and dinners. The adjoining village hall restaurant offers a self-service buffet between April and October.

How to get there: Stourton village, Stourhead House and Stourhead Gardens lie just off the B3092 Frome to Mere road, about 10 miles south of Frome. With Stourhead being one of the National Trust's most famous properties, the location is well signposted for several miles around. Just after turning off the B3092, there is a large National Trust car-park on the left-hand side as you enter Stourton. (GR 778341)

The Walk: From the National Trust's car-park, follow the signs that point you to Stourhead House. An impressive gateway leads into the grounds, whilst your walk passes through the rather more humble – but certainly more interesting – old turnstile to its right. Beyond the turnstile continue along the made-up footpath, with the imposing eastern front of Stourhead House away to the left. In less than ½ mile, a small gate marks the exit from the parkland onto the Kilmington road.

Immediately opposite is a stile, beyond which you follow a field-path. The route is not made up, but it is well used and relatively easy to follow. Basically, continue straight ahead and when the ground begins to slope downwards look ahead for some vertical poles that represent the corner of the field. Beyond this point, continue across the next field to a stile, all the while keeping the field boundary to your immediate right.

The stile brings you to a marvellous sunken path, but it is worth pausing to take one last look at the fine view you will have enjoyed since crossing the Kilmington road. To the east lies White Sheet Hill, north-eastwards rises Cold Kitchen Hill and neighbouring Brimsdown Hill, whilst to the north are the prominent hillocks known as Long and Little Knoll.

Turn left along a track which is actually the course of an old coach road that ran from Salisbury to the West Country until the 19th century. In ½ mile you emerge at a crossroads, where the ramble continues straight ahead, following the lane signposted to Alfred's Tower. There is at this point a short section of road walking, but the absence of trees makes for an open vista. The hedgerows are delightful, festooned with all those plants and flowers that are so much a part of the English landscape – honeysuckle, foxglove, hawthorn, bramble and a host more besides. The lane eventually passes into the trees, and it is not long before you turn right onto a farm track. A barn and assorted sheds mark this junction.

Continue along this track across open arable fields until it enters King's Wood Warren. Very shortly the path comes face to face with Cox's Lodge, (circa 1845). Take the path to the left, cross the stile, and enter the heart of the woodland.

Ignore the path to the right, which turns off soon after the stile, instead continue straight ahead through relatively dense tree-cover. Shortly, the path joins a woodland track, the trees have been cleared, and young conifers planted in their place. This absence of mature cover means far-ranging views westwards over tracts of east Somerset.

Continue along the forester's track, taking the left fork at the next junction. In about ½ mile there is one further fork where your route again lies to the left, continuing beyond the single-barred wooden gate. Beyond this point, it is but another ½ mile onto the country lane that drops steeply down Kingsettle Hill from Wiltshire into Somerset.

It is worth climbing the bank on the right of the path just before you reach the road to enjoy the fine view westwards, especially if Alfred's Tower is going to be closed. Turn left, climb Kingsettle Hill and at the top cut through the gap in the hedge on the right-hand side. Rising dramatically in front of you is Alfred's Tower, and if it is open a toll will gain you access to its 222 steps and a huge view of much of eastern Somerset. Otherwise, you will be disappointed for this is a tree-covered hilltop with no alternative viewpoint.

There are several pathways into the woods around Alfred's Tower, but only one of them will return you to Stourton. The others will provide fine woodland walks, but in all probability you will end up back at the Tower – believe me, I speak from experience!

Continue along the grassed area in front of the Tower. There is a path on the right alongside the National Trust's parking area, but this is not your path. A little further on, again on the right, a pair of paths enter the trees – again, this is not your route. At the far end of the grassed enclosure, with tree-cover embracing you on all sides, the pathway into the woods is the route to Stourton. Just check that entry to the woods is via a single-barred wooden gate, and look for the sign warning owners not to unleash their dogs onto the local deer population, and you can be sure that you are not destined for a 2-hour circular ramble through the woods!

Take the path to the left (there is a less distinct track bearing to the right) and continue down through the trees for little over a mile. The well-defined track eventually emerges into an open field, and the only obvious route brings you between the dam of the lake in Stourhead Gardens and Turner's Paddock Lake. On the far banks of the lake is a rather beautiful man-made cascade.

Beyond the lake join a road, where a left-turn takes you under a rocky arched bridge into the village of Stourton, the Gardens to your left, the church to the right. Continue along the lane if you wish to return immediately to the NT car-park where the walk began. Otherwise stay to enjoy the delights of one of England's most famous landscaped gardens.

Historical Notes

The Stourhead Estate: Henry Hoare I, a wealthy London banker, bought the Manor of Stourton in 1718, demolished the old Stourton House, and in its place erected an imposing Palladian mansion, Stourhead House. The House contains a fine collection of art treasures, which include paintings by Gainsborough, Reynolds, Canaletto and Raphael, as well as some items of furniture constructed by Thomas Chippendale the younger on the Stourhead premises.

Stourhead Gardens are quite rightly ranked as one of the most famous landscaped gardens in the world. What was once a series of medieval fishponds was transformed in the

18th century by Henry Hoare II into one of the earliest idyllic landscapes in England. A lake is the central focus, surrounded by classical temples, bridges and rustic grottos, rare specimens of trees and plants, and a steady succession of flowers that add beauty throughout the seasons. The Hoare family gave the Stourhead Estate to the National Trust in 1946, since when its character and atmosphere have been carefully maintained.

Selwood Forest, ancient and primeval, at one time swept in a mighty arc southwards from Bath deep into the heart of Dorset. Literally 'the wood of sallows', the name is indicative of the waterlogged nature of the terrain at that time. Between Stourton and Alfred's Tower the walk passes through vestiges of this once great forest. This natural frontier checked the westward progress of successive waves of invaders, from the Celts and the Romans to the Saxons.

Alfred's Tower, high on Somerset's eastern boundary, was designed by Henry Flitcroft. The inscription on the tablet at Arthur's Tower suggests that it marks the spot where Alfred rallied his troops before the victory over the Danes at Ethandune in AD 879. Whether the tower marks the actual spot where 'there came unto him all the men of Somerset, and the Wiltshire men, and of the Hampshire men such as were yet on this side of the water' is a matter for some conjecture. It is perhaps more realistic to follow the line that the tower was in fact built to mark peace with France and the succession of George III in 1760. The triangular brick structure is impressive by any standards. It stands 160 feet in height, its crenellated parapet standing over 1,000 feet above sea-level. The interior is hollow and open to the sky, whilst at each corner of the triangle is a round tower, one of which contains the 222 steps that convey the visitor to its summit.

The tower is open on Wednesday, Thursday, Saturday and Sunday afternoons between April and October.

17

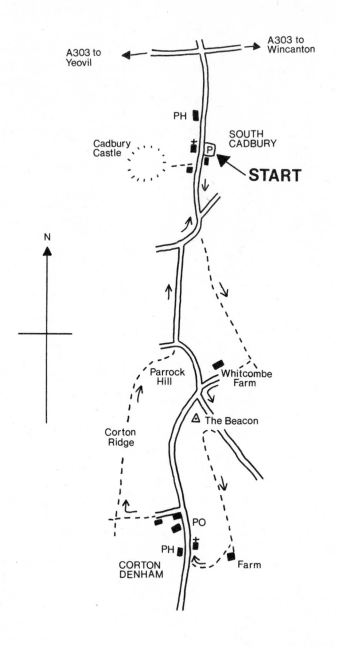

In Search of Arthur's Camelot: Cadbury Castle

Introduction: Deep in the heart of south Somerset, almost on the Dorset border, lies one of the most exciting antiquities in the whole of the county – South Cadbury Castle, to many the site of Arthur's Camelot. It stands as the northern outpost of an area of fine hill country, where the slopes drop, cliff-like, to the sea of the Central Plain. Corton Ridge, Corton Hill, The Beacon, Windmill Hill, Wheatsheaf Hill – the names on the map are indicative of this beautiful slice of landscape. Cadbury Castle, however, is what the visitors come to see. Its steep, thickly-wooded sides rise to a wide flat plateau almost a mile round, enclosed by four circles of great grassy ramparts. It is a fine vantage point which for centuries has looked out across the surrounding countryside. Sometimes, what was seen brought anxiety and terror, on other occasions triumph, whilst to today's visitor the most common feeling is one of pure contentment.

Distance: This is a 5½ mile circuit, with an extra mile or so at the end for the almost compulsory climb onto Cadbury Castle.

Refreshments: In South Cadbury, a few hundred yards from the start of the walk, there is the *Red Lion Inn*. In Corton Denham, conveniently situated half-way around the ramble, we find the *Queen's Arms*, and the post office selling confectionery.

How to get there: South Cadbury lies just south of the A303 trunk road from London to the West Country. The minor road into the village lies 6 miles west of Wincanton. Continue through South Cadbury to the village church, outside which there is room for careful roadside parking. (GR 632255)

The Walk: South Cadbury church is the starting point for this ramble. Continue southwards out of the village, passing Castle Lane to your right. 50 yards beyond the junction with Crang's Lane cross the stile on the left-hand side. Head directly across the paddock beyond to another stile beneath a fine old oak tree, cross the stile and follow the left-hand boundary of an arable field.

At the end of this field you will reach a track, which you leave as it bears left to enter the field directly ahead. Yet again follow the field boundary. At the far corner of this field cross a fence and an open vista looms ahead. Hills all around, Whitcombe Farm half-right, hidden behind hedgerows and trees, beyond which rises the inviting Beacon Hill. The farm and the beacon are, in fact, your next targets.

Follow the field boundary ahead for 800 yards, walking on the rough scrubland at the foot of the hill, and keeping the fence to the right. At the end this time, an enclosed track is followed to the right, which brings you out onto the road beyond Whitcombe Farm. (Incidentally, you can reach the same point by means of 1½ miles of road walking from South Cadbury. This option is shown on the map.)

Turn left, and almost immediately left again, to climb Beacon Lane. At its summit, you will pass a clump of pine trees on the right-hand side. Just beyond this point, there is a gateway on the right where you enter the hilltop fields and head for the beacon directly ahead. A fine view awaits you. To the south-east lie the Blackdown Hills, westwards lies Yeovil and the Yeovilton airfield, to the north are laid out the Mendip Hills, and, of course, almost on the doorstep is

Cadbury Castle. Beneath lies the village of Corton Denham, your next target.

Head off along the hilltop, gateways indicating the route of the right-of-way, until ½ mile ahead New Barn Farm appears in front of you. Before reaching the farm, the path drops to pass through a gate in the fence that slopes down the hillside. Continue on the right-hand path downhill to the village, a stile bringing you onto a short stretch of lane that leads into the village High Street. A most pleasant place Corton Denham is, too. Mellow cottages and friendly faces, lots of 'good mornings' over garden gates in what seems a traditional village community.

Continue along the High Street, where there are three tempting diversions. Firstly, the *Queen's Arms* on the left. Secondly, St Andrew's church, further along on the right. Finally, the village post office, purveyor of soft drinks and confectionery.

Almost on the northern outskirts of the village, turn left to follow a cul-de-sac lane that passes Yew Tree Farm before gradually climbing the hillside to reach Corton Ridge. Where the track ends, cross the gate directly ahead, turn sharp right and follow the western side of the ridge for ½ mile towards Parrock Hill. Yet again, magnificent views are your constant companion.

The path passes around the western side of the hill, before following a short enclosed track down to the road. Follow the turning opposite signposted to South Cadbury, turning right at the first junction and forking left where Church Lane and Crang's Lane diverge. It is but a few minutes back to South Cadbury where the walk began.

Cadbury Castle is never out of sight during this last mile of road-walking, so it is only fitting that at the end of the walk you should climb Castle Lane to explore the mile of ramparts of what many consider to be the legendary Camelot. And not too far away to the north-east lies the site that could well be Avalon, Glastonbury Tor, Arthur's fortress and Arthur's grave. In centuries past, these two landmarks would have been separated by the flooded Levels, two secret islands in a mysterious sea! Arthur's dying frame would have been taken by water to its resting place:

'Then murmur'd Arthur, "Place me in the barge."
So to the barge they came. There those three Queens
Put forth their hands, and took the King and wept.'

Historical Notes

South Cadbury Church is dedicated to St Thomas à Becket, martyred at Canterbury in 1170. A finely restored wall-painting of a bishop in a cope and mitre adorns the splay of a window in the south aisle, and is commonly felt to represent St Thomas. The 14th century tower, complete with a turret and pinnacles, makes the church a notable local landmark, whether approached from the north or the south, and closer inspection reveals its corner buttresses and gargoyles. The arcade of the church is part of the original Early English building, dating from about 1280. Like most Somerset churches, however, South Cadbury was largely rebuilt in the Perpendicular style. Within the churchyard are three fine trees – a tulip, a yew and a ginkgo – as well as many fine old gravestones. An interesting note in the church guide records that the playing of 'fives' against the church wall was stopped in 1771 – at least the tradition is still kept alive at Eton and Rugby, if not at South Cadbury!

Cadbury Castle is, like Old Sarum and Maiden Castle, a site of multi-occupancy over many epochs of human civilisation. Neolithic people originally populated the hilltop. During the Iron Age the vast system of banks and ditches was constructed, the Romans established Cadbury as a fortified station from which to subjugate the hostile Britons, whilst Ethelred the Unready reinforced the innermost rampart around AD 1000 in anticipation of Danish invaders.

It is the Arthurian legends that draw visitors to Cadbury,

for this is indeed said to be the site of Camelot. Proving any association is almost impossible, and with Glastonbury and 'Avalon' so close at hand it was inevitable that this hilltop with its 'green, silent and fairly tense' atmosphere should be drawn into the tales of Arthur. However, one piece of supporting evidence must be quoted. Major excavations were carried out at Cadbury between 1966 and 1970, chiefly to establish whether the site was occupied by an important chieftain at an appropriate date. The digs proved without a shadow of doubt that this great hill-camp was refortified and re-used about AD 500, with the evidence suggesting that the site was occupied by a chieftain of considerable importance, education and wealth. It was a project that bore 'the stamp of a bold, original but still anonymous mind'. Arthur, it must be remembered, was a legendary English 'king' and hero of the 6th century AD.

Corton Denham Church had become so dilapidated and inadequate for its congregation that it was literally taken down in March 1869 and rebuilt. As well as a fine new building, the parishioners got an extra 50 seats and a recast large bell, courtesy of Messrs Warner of London. The new building was consecrated by the Bishop of Bath and Wells on 26th July 1870. The contractors, Messrs Draper and Trask, charged £2,685 for their labours, which strikes me as something of a bargain! The contents of the new church – items like the roof carving, the stained windows and the heating apparatus – cost an additional £725, an expense that was generously defrayed by the Rector. The church obviously dates back a long way before 1869, its first recorded date being 1267 when a certain Hugh Monteforti was the first incumbent. Little is known of the earlier building, the church records – dating from 1538 – recording important items such as the weather and recipes for dog bites, but nothing incidental like church architecture!

Montacute and Ham Hill

Introduction: Montacute is strategically sited on the old Exeter to London coach-road, and a delightful village for an overnight stop it would have been too! Its square, known as The Borough, is surrounded by picturesque houses that over the years must have witnessed many annual fairs and dealings by traders in leather and wool. Just beyond the square lies what most visitors come to see – Montacute House. This Elizabethan mansion, one of the most famous great houses of Somerset, contains amongst its many attractions the largest long gallery in England. Whether in the village or whether visiting the House, it is the stone that creates the abiding impression, the golden stone, described by Pevsner as 'soft biscuit to a tanned tone'. It is 'ham stone', quarried from Ham Hill, whose vast hilltop rises above Montacute. This ramble takes us from the mellow streets of the village, onto the ramparts of the hillfort atop Ham Hill. Everywhere the land surface is pitted, the result of centuries of quarrying activity that produced one of Britain's most famous building materials.

N.B. A muddy patch is almost certain to be encountered on this walk so appropriate footwear should be worn.

Distance: This is a 5½ mile circuit, where a good 3 hours will be filled if the views from Ham Hill are to be fully appreciated. The actual village of Montacute, including the House, would easily take a further couple of hours to explore.

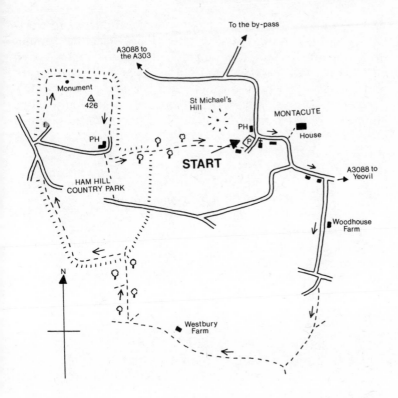

Refreshments: At the start of the walk, alongside the church, is the *King's Arms*. In The Borough, there is the *Phelip's Arms* as well as the Tudor Rose tea-rooms. Outside Montacute, and on the actual ramble, the *Prince of Wales* public house, high on top of Ham Hill, is probably the only hostelry lying within the ramparts of a hillfort.

How to get there: Montacute lies on the A3088 road linking Yeovil with the A303. There is room for careful parking in the side road between the church and the *Kings Arms*, just a short distance west of the entrance to Montacute House. (GR 497169)

The Walk: The walk begins with ½ mile of pavement walking, but it is through the delightful village streets of Montacute. From St Catherine's church follow the main Yeovil road, fortunately a beneficiary of a recent by-pass. It is not long before you pass through The Borough, Montacute's version of a town square, surrounded by houses and shops built of golden stone. Continue along the main road until, just beyond a garage on the edge of the village, a lane turns off on the right-hand side. An isolated house overlooks the junction.

Follow this lane uphill for ½ mile, passing Woodhouse Farm as the lungs move into top gear, turn left at the hilltop junction, and almost immediately turn right to follow a farm lane. In less than 200 yards, leave the lane to continue along an enclosed bridleway through the trees to the left.

In ½ mile, turn right to follow another enclosed track down Hocker's Hill for close on a mile. There are occasional left and right turns, all of which should be ignored, until you reach the foot of the hill below Westbury Farm. Here you do turn right to follow a track uphill through Norton Covert, signposted to Ham Hill. Ignore the first left turn halfway up the hill, turning left instead at the hilltop where you follow an overgrown path beneath the southern-most ramparts of the Ham Hill Fort.

Continue along this path, trees, bushes and bracken initially blocking all views. Eventually, gaps do occur in the hedgerow, and wide views extending across Norton-sub-Hamdon and South Somerset to the Blackdown Hills open up. There are several tempting right turns, but keep to the main path that borders the perimeter of the hilltop. That is actually a good principle for the whole of the walk around Ham Hill. Almost inconspicuously, the path turns to head northwards, and the views are now to the west. There are no particular landmarks, it is simply an extremely far-ranging rural view.

Very soon you join Ham Hill Road where you turn left, passing a car-parking area just beyond a road junction, and continue along the hilltop road in the direction signposted 'Prince of Wales Public House First Right'.

Take that first right, almost immediately fork left, and again almost immediately leave the road to follow a footpath on the left signposted to 'The Monument and Stoke-sub-Hamdon'. The path continues along the western edge of Ham Hill until, when the War Memorial appears, bear right onto the northern ramparts. The views from the Memorial to the north are superb – laid out below are the Somerset Levels, beyond which rise the Mendip Hills. Particular landmarks are Glastonbury Tor, and Pen Hill Mast on the Mendips above Wells.

Continue to the end of the northern ramparts, bear right and follow the eastern side of the hilltop on to the *Prince of Wales*. It can be a tricky business getting back to Montacute from the inn, and not for the reasons you're thinking! The hilltop is riddled with old quarrying pits, and paths appear everywhere.

Firstly, turn the corner by the *Prince of Wales*, and pass through a gap in the hedge on the left signposted to 'Montacute'. (The easy way back is simply to head directly across the quarried ground in front to the road, turn left and in just over a mile you will be in Montacute, just east of The Borough. There is one fork in the road en route where you bear left.)

There is also a footpath back to the village. Beyond the gap in the hedge, bear left and head for the far left-hand corner of the quarried hilltop. Follow the path into the trees, and gradually descend back to Montacute. In ½ mile, cross a stile into an open field, pass to the right of St Michael's Hill, continue along the path back to Abbey Farm and turn left along the lane back to the church where the walk began.

Historical Notes

Montacute House is a large Elizabethan mansion built of the warm local Ham Hill stone. It was commissioned by Sir

27

Edward Phelips, Speaker of the House of Commons and Master of the Rolls, in the 1590s and completed in 1601. Montacute is perhaps best-loved for its pure symmetry of design, being constructed to a regular H-shaped plan and surrounded by formal gardens of old roses and yew hedgerows. The House contains fine collections of 16th and 17th century paintings, furnishings, and tapestries, and 18th century ceramics. The Long Gallery, all 189 feet of it, is reputedly the longest in England, and houses 16th and 17th century Elizabethan and Jacobean portraits on loan from the National Gallery.

St Michael's Hill, originally 'mons acutus' or the 'pointed hill', points the way to the origins of the name 'Montacute'. It was acquired by Robert, the Count of Mortain, after the Norman Conquest, and he fortified the hilltop by means of a castle. This act was a savage blow to the subjugated English to whom the hill was a holy place akin to Glastonbury. The hill was held in great awe due to mystical happenings there in the days of King Canute. Tofig, his standard-bearer, was fired with a vision that demanded he climb the hill with his priest and dig into its soil. The pair came across a great stone which was 'cleft in twain' before their very eyes to reveal a glistening black flint crucifix. This was loaded onto a wagon and hauled by 12 red oxen and 12 white cows, destination sacred but unknown! It proceeded to Essex, and came to a halt in the village of Waltham. This was hallowed ground, and an Abbey was built around the Holy Cross. King Harold is said to have prayed before the relic prior to the Norman invasion in 1066 but to no apparent avail!

Ham Hill is a tremendous fortified settlement that rises impressively above the surrounding Central Plain. The L-shaped hillfort, originally built by Iron Age settlers, is encompassed by 3 miles of ramparts enclosing a site of some 200 acres. A strategic site, overlooking the Fosse Way, excavations have revealed evidence of a 12-roomed villa together with artefacts ranging from a chariot wheel and brooches to weaving implements and toilet articles. It was the Romans who also recognised the beauty of the warm golden-yellow Ham Hill stone, and commenced quarrying activities on the hilltop. These continued right through to the 1960s, when the United Stone Firms Limited – successor to the Ham Hill & Doulting Stone Co – finally worked out the last of the economic beds of shelly limestone. The stone is unique, so much so that when nearby Barrington Court was undergoing repairs in 1968, local disused railway bridges had to be plundered for the necessary hamstone, the quarries having ceased operations by this time.

The remains of the quarried hilltop have left a natural adventure playground, so it is not surprising to see that the County Council have created a Country Park from the site.

The Abbey Farmhouse, passed at the end of the walk, was one of the last buildings to be erected by the Clunic monks who lived in the local monastery. The monastery was founded by the Count of Mortain, allegedly to atone for his earlier sacrilege upon St Michael's Hill. Unfortunately, the Dissolution of the Monasteries by Henry VIII largely destroyed the complex of monastic buildings. The Borough, Montacute's square, owes its origins to the expanding monastery's need for a market-place, where leather and wool could be traded, whilst the farmhouse was the gateway to the monastery beyond. It carries the initials of Thomas Chard, Prior between 1514 and 1532. Beyond the House, and with public footpath access, lie the monks' trout-pond and a dovecot, the only other relics of what the OS map describes as 'Priory – remains of'.

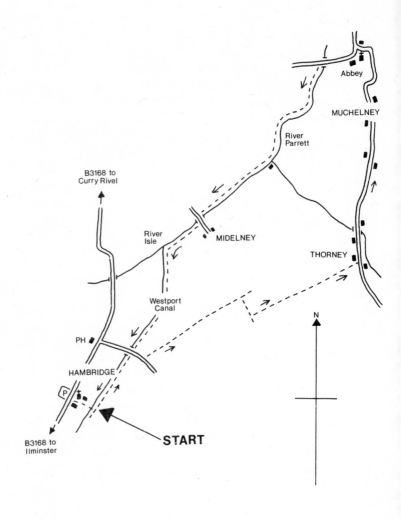

Abbey

MUCHELNEY

River
Parrett

B3168 to
Curry Rivel

River
Isle

MIDELNEY

THORNEY

Westport
Canal

N

PH

HAMBRIDGE

P

START

B3168 to
Ilminster

Muchelney Abbey and the Levels

Introduction: Deep in the heartlands of Somerset lies the fascinating land of the Somerset Levels. Mile after mile of drove roads and tracks where contour lines appear to have been omitted from the map. The network of rivers, canals and rhines that drain the Levels provide a unique environment for the botanist, the ornithologist and the naturalist. The waterways are lined with willow, the rhines with yellow flag and sedge. Herons and moorhens beat an indignant retreat in the face of intruders upon their territory, whilst the dragonflies continue on regardless. Muchelney, literally the 'big island', rises above this landscape being 25–30 feet above sea-level! The Abbey is second only to Glastonbury in terms of the county's religious antiquities, the nearby Priest's House lies scarcely altered since the 14th century, whilst the village can boast the workshops of a potter of international repute.

Distance: An 8 mile ramble across flat countryside where the going is very straightforward. Allow approximately 3 hours.

Refreshments: Half a mile north of Hambridge church, on the B3168 road back to Curry Rivel, there is the *Lamb and Lion* public house. On the B3168 south of the church, in the neighbouring village of Westport, there is the *Old Barn Owl Inn*. There are no refreshment facilities on the walk itself.

How to get there: The walk starts at Hambridge church, which lies 3 miles south of Curry Rivel on the B3168 road to

Ilminster. There is room for careful parking outside the church. (GR 393210)

The Walk: To the south of the church, follow the path on the left that passes in front of the Parish Rooms. This path continues in front of a cottage, before passing between a pair of high hedgerows to reach a gate. Cross the paddock ahead, keeping to the right-hand field boundary, head directly across the next field to a gap in the hedgerow, beyond which a quaint old footbridge crosses the Westport Canal to reach the towpath. Follow the towpath to the left for a little over ½ mile, until you reach a country lane that runs from Hambridge to Stembridge.

Follow the lane to the right for no more than 100 yards, before turning left onto an old drove track across the levels. This track is followed for over ½ mile to a junction, where you should bear right along the flat treeless path ahead. Three particular landmarks stand out: to the right, with its clump of trees, is the nearby Higher Burrow Hill; ahead, and several miles off, is Ham Hill with its prominent obelisk; to the left the Perpendicular tower of Kingsbury Episcopi church, all 99 feet of it, rises prominently above the Levels.

In less than ¼ mile, turn left onto a final drove track which is followed for a mile onto the road at Thorney. Before reaching Thorney, one or two fine waterways are crossed – it is hard to distinguish between rivers, rhines and canals on the Levels – where the rushes and yellow flag, the mallard and the heron, are ever-present. The land is chiefly used for cattle and sheep grazing, although there is an occasional osier copse.

Turn left at the road to pass through the small hamlet of Thorney. This is a nice mixture of whitewash and thatch, redbrick and slate, and stone and tile, a real rural community judging by the number of over-the-wall vendors of everything ranging from peat and marrows, to plants and herbs!

Continue along the road for just over a mile to Muchelney. (I was fascinated to see a huge sign alongside one field advertising it to be the site of the 'Lowland Games' that August, where competitors would engage in raft races, river sports, tug-o-war, terrier racing and clay-pigeon shooting.)

There are three separate parts to Muchelney. The first to be reached is the group of houses that includes John Leach the potter's workshop. The pottery was established here in 1964, and exhibitions of its work have been held as far afield as the United States and Japan. The second group of buildings, grouped around the Old School House, would appear to be the heart of the village community, whilst the northern end of the village is 'visitors' Muchelney', the abbey ruins, the church and the Priest's House. Outside the church is a small green that houses the village cross.

Take the turning to the left, signposted to 'Drayton and Curry Rivel', and in less than ¼ mile you will cross the river Parrett. Immediately, turn left and follow the banks of the river, following the path signposted 'Midelney Bridge 1¾'.

Within a mile, you will reach the pumping station at the confluence of the Parrett with the Isle, whose banks are followed for ½ mile to Midelney Bridge. (A detour along the lane into Midelney will bring you to the local manor house.)

At Midelney Bridge, the footpath changes river banks and it is but ¼ mile to the junction of the Isle with the Westport Canal. Bear left to follow the canal towpath for 1½ miles back to that rickety old footbridge and the path to Hambridge church where the walk began, probably unsettling several solitary herons on the way!

Historical Notes

The Westport Canal The river Parrett had always been one of Somerset's major navigations, linking Bridgwater, Langport and much of central Somerset with the Bristol Channel. It remained unimproved until 1836, when the Parrett Navigation Company was formed to fight off the competition from the nearby Chard Canal. Locks were installed on the river, an ancient bridge at Langport was demolished and rebuilt to allow for easier passage of vessels, and a 2½ mile extension of the waterway was constructed to the village of Westport. Among the backers of the project were the Stuckeys and the Bagehots, two families of merchants and bankers, who dominated the local economy in the 18th and 19th centuries. The canal was wide and capricious, guaranteeing 4 feet of water to vessels, and it thrived for a few decades until the inevitable competition from the railways. Traffic lingered on through the 1870s: coal, slate, salt, bricks and drainpipes coming into Westport; elm timber, willows, flax, wheat and cider being shipped out; – until the inevitable cessation of traffic shortly after the closure of the Parrett Navigation in 1878.

Today the canal is in remarkably good repair. The bed holds water throughout its course, and is followed by a fine towpath. The whole waterway has become a haven for wildlife and moisture-loving plants. At the end of the walk, it is worth driving (or continuing on foot!) the short distance into Westport to see the canal's terminal limbs, with their solid warehousing and offices still standing and virtually intact. The complex lies just to the south of the village inn, and can be viewed from a track that crosses the canal opposite a turning to Isle Brewers.

Muchelney Abbey was destroyed during the Dissolution of the Monasteries, with today's remains essentially consisting of little more than the ground plan. The abbey was established in the 8th century by Benedictine monks, with popular tradition believing its founder to be the Wessex King Ine. An alternative explanation suggests that the Abbey was founded by King Athelstan to commemorate the victory of Brunanburgh in AD 937.

Muchelney literally means 'big island', a name derived from the fact that the village stands a few feet higher than the surrounding Levels. Before the Dissolution, this would have made the abbey a most prominent local landmark. It was never a large establishment, 20 monks being the maximum recorded at the abbey, with only 10 remaining in 1539. After the Dissolution the building's masonry apparently became fair game for the local villagers, and it is an intriguing task to spot the finials and carvings that now adorn local cottages and farmhouses. One story even suggests that the Abbey's south cloister became a cider store! Opposite the village church – most noted for its naive 17th century ceiling paintings depicting buxom cherubs floating on cotton-wool clouds – is the Priest's House. This is a delightful survival from the monastic days, a late medieval two-storeyed thatched cottage, with a fine two-centred doorway and a four-light transom-window. Despite its lack of size, this dwelling is modelled upon the designs of a large mansion. Fortunately, the Priest's House is a National Trust property, and can be viewed internally. The actual village of Muchelney is a true delight.

Midelney Manor was originally the island manor of the Abbots of Muchelney. Since the Dissolution of the Monasteries, it has been in the hands of the Trevilian family. The Elizabethan house that we see today was originally built by two Trevilian brothers, one to have exclusive use of the left half, the other of the right! A two-storey building, it originally had gabled dormers in the roof. Today's building has two doorways, mullioned windows with hoodmoulds and two gabled projecting wings. Inside the Manor, which is open on Wednesday afternoons in the summer months, there is Georgian and Louis XV furniture, porcelain and armorial china, paintings and family mementoes including High Sheriff's banners. Behind the house, in the flower-filled gardens, is a rare survival – an 18th century Falcons' Mews built of brick with stone dressings.

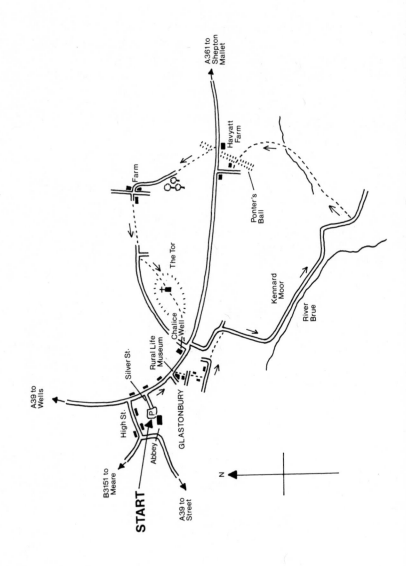

Glastonbury Tor: 'Avalon'

Introduction: The mystical land of Avalon has had long and romantic associations with Glastonbury and the famous Tor. In Celtic legend, Avalon was the 'island of the blest' or 'paradise', whilst in Arthurian legend it was the 'land of heroes' to which the dead king was conveyed. Although no longer surrounded by lake and marshland, the massive hillock rising out of the early morning mist as it blankets the surrounding Levels is indeed reminiscent of a mysterious island silhouetted against the Somerset sky. The Tor dominates this ramble. Out on the lonely Levels, there she lies as a permanent backdrop. As we retrace our steps towards Glastonbury, she rises as a daunting, but nonetheless compelling, landmark whose summit *must* be secured simply because it is there. For others, to climb the Tor is altogether a more mystical experience.

Distance: This ramble covers some 6 miles. With the ascent of the Tor left for the end of the walk, a good 3 hours should be allowed so that this fine vantage point over much of Somerset can be fully enjoyed.

Refreshments: The walk starts and finishes in Glastonbury, where every conceivable taste is catered for. If you prefer a packed lunch, there can be few better spots than the Tor for a picnic.

How to get there: Glastonbury lies on the A39 Bath to Minehead road. As you approach the town centre from Wells, rather than bearing right into the High Street, continue straight on along the A361 signposted to Shepton

Mallet. Almost immediately, there is a right turn into Silver Street where you will find a local authority car-park. If you have problems locating Silver Street, it lies between the High Street and the Abbey Walls. (GR 502389)

The Walk: From the car-park, walk back up Silver Street alongside the boundary wall of the abbey. Turn right at the junction with Chilkwell Street, and continue along this busy road to a mini-roundabout where Bere Lane joins from the right. Cross Chilkwell Street with great care at this busy junction, and turn right down the footpath alongside Abbey Barn, which now houses a museum of rural life. The barn and adjoining Victorian farmhouse are on the right-hand side as you pass down the path to reach a new housing development.

Follow the tarmac footpaths due south through the estate, crossing Actis Road, until you reach the lower boundary road of the housing development. Turn left along this road, and where it bears to the left, cross the stile on your right into an open field. From the busy hustle-and-bustle of Glastonbury, you are now heading out into the lonely spaces of the Somerset Levels, out onto Kennard Moor to be precise.

Follow the left-hand hedgerow of the field onto Plunging Drove, where you turn right and continue to Plunging, a medieval ford through the river Brue. The lane bears to the left, becoming Kennard Moor Drove, and your route borders the Brue for some distance.

Half a mile after the lane leaves the riverside, look for a large drove on the left, reached through an iron cattle stockade. Follow the drove to reach Coxbridge brook, then turn right along the river bank until you reach Clyce Corner. A detour to the right to find a bridge across the rhine is necessary, before you return to Clyce Corner only on the opposite bank of the water.

Continue across the field to a gate, cross the next field to another gate, and then half-left across the next field to reach

Ponter's Ball earthworks. This strange linear bank, about one mile in length with a ditch on its eastern side, has obscure origins. It was possibly part of an outer defence system surrounding the sites of Glastonbury, or could it have been the quayside where vessels berthed on reaching the Isle of Avalon?

The stile alongside Ponter's Ball indicates that the field-path continues straight ahead, passing to the left of Havyatt Farm to emerge onto a track. Turn right, and very shortly you will meet the traffic on the busy A361 Glastonbury to Shepton Mallet road. After the tranquillity of the Levels, with its rhines and wildlife, the noise of the lorries and vans and commercial vehicles is an unpleasant shock!

Cross the A361, and continue eastwards (i.e. to the right) along the pavement for a short distance. Just opposite Havyatt Farm, a fieldpath goes off on the left, signposted alongside a gateway. Your target is the large group of farm buildings, Norwood Park Farm, some ½ mile distant. To reach them, proceed half-left across the open fields in front of you towards the trees ahead. Fine views of Glastonbury Tor can be seen to the left. Alongside the trees, join a farm lane that is followed up the slight rise to the farm buildings ahead. Pass around the buildings, and out onto the quiet country lane beyond.

Continue on up the enclosed track in front of a rank of farm cottages, in the general direction of the Tor. The track climbs quite steeply up the hillside to eventually become a tarmac lane. At the top of the lane – Stone Down Lane – enter the official National Trust entrance to the Tor. I can assure you that the ascent of the Tor to reach the ruined tower of St Michael's church has not been deliberately left until the end as some sort of punishment! It is a stiff climb, but the reward is one vast 360 degree panorama across much of Somerset. A convenient topograph pinpoints the various landmarks, always assuming that the surrounding Levels are not blanketed in a sea of mist.

Once you have had your fill of the fine views, descend the

far side of the Tor along the obvious pathway to emerge onto the lower end of Wellhouse Lane. Continue down to the main road, and turn right to head back into Glastonbury. On your right, you will pass the entrance to the Chalice Well gardens, before reaching the mini-roundabout at the junction of Chilkwell Street and Bere Lane. As this spot was passed very early on in the walk, it is an easy matter to find your way back to the Silver Street car-park; unless you first wish to cross the road and visit the Country Life Museum!

Historical Notes

Glastonbury Abbey is but a shadow of its former glory, following the Dissolution of the Monasteries in the 16th century. Abbot Richard Whiting, reputedly the 60th Abbot of Glastonbury, was dragged upon a hurdle to the top of the nearby Tor and hung on 15th November 1539. His body was quartered, and the inhabitants of Bath, Wells, Bridgwater and Ilchester were treated to an exhibition of the dismembered parts! The Abbot's death was the signal for the wholesale ransacking of the abbey to begin. The roof was stripped of its lead, carved wooden screens were used as fuel for the smelting process, and ancient manuscripts bundled up as kindling. The fine stone which had been quarried at nearby Doulting, was sold as job-lots to local builders.

In its prime, this was indeed a vast abbey, whose length of 594 feet exceeded that of Wells cathedral by more than 200 feet.

It is impossible to do justice to the vast history and traditions of the abbey in just a few sentences. Visitors really should pay the entrance fee, purchase the guide-book and visit this legendary place for themselves.

The Somerset Levels: In centuries past, the flat, low-lying land around Glastonbury Tor would have been one vast area of marsh, a land of reeds, rushes and sedge, meandering creeks and isolated pools. It was not until the Middle Ages that drainage of the Levels began, at the behest of the Abbot of Glastonbury. Today the Levels, or the 'Moors' as they are known locally, provide a fascinating landscape. The fields are bounded by deep ditches, known as 'rhines', and often lined with pollarded willow trees. Peat extraction is widely practised across the Levels, whilst more locally basketware is produced from the willow. The area is renowned for its birdlife, and is especially important for waders, having the south-west of England's largest lowland concentration of lapwing, snipe, redshank and curlew. For a useful introduction to the Levels, its history, crafts and wildlife, it is worth visiting the Peat Moor Visitors Centre on the Shapwick to Westhay road near Glastonbury.

Glastonbury Tor has a dominance that belies its mere 520 feet of height. This conical-shaped hill rises from the excessively horizontal local landscape to catch the eye of even the most unobservant traveller. Like that other landmark, Brent Knoll, clearly visible less than 20 miles to the west, the Tor is simply a harder lias core from which the softer rock has been worn away. The ruined tower that dominates the hilltop is that of the 14th century St Michael's church, an earlier satellite monastic settlement on the hilltop having been destroyed by either a landslide or an earthquake in 1275. The Tor was the site of the local gibbet – for example, Abbot Richard Whiting, the last Abbot of Glastonbury, met his end here in 1539.

The facts are dry, the myths legendary. This was supposedly the entrance to the Underworld, the Kingdom of Annwn. Gwyn-ap Nudd, its king, had his invisible palace guarding the entrance. The terraces that spiral the hill were said to be man-made, a circular maze to the palace, and the hill itself was a hollow, human creation. It is unfortunate for the romantics that Glastonbury Tor is just one of many hills in south-east Somerset with hillside terraces, perhaps strip-lynchets or former vineyards.

41

The Chalice Well is a natural spring whose daily flow of 25,000 gallons of water provided Glastonbury with its main water supply until the 19th century. As with so much else in the locality, the well has its mythical connotations. It is allegedly known as the Chalice Well because Joseph of Aramathea was said to have hidden the Chalice Cup of the Last Supper beneath its waters. With the Chalice Cup being the Holy Grail of Arthurian Legend, the site has become a sacred and mystical place. Its red waters have earned it the title of 'Blood Spring', although the colour is in reality due to the waters flowing through iron deposits, perhaps beneath the nearby Mendip Hills, rather than the presence of the Holy Grail! Certainly, a cupful of the water leaves a significant metallic taste in the mouth. The Well is set amongst a beautiful terraced garden, and is tended by a private Trust. The very modest admission fee is worth every penny to savour the unique atmosphere of this lovely spot.

The Abbey Barn, the 14th century home barn of Glastonbury Abbey, has been open to the public since 1976 as the home of the Somerset Rural Life Museum. The complex also includes the adjoining Victorian farmhouse. The barn's interior roof structure, described by experts as a 'two-tier cruck design', vividly displays the skills of the medieval carpenter. Following its restoration, this fine structure – 93 feet long and 33 feet wide – was reroofed in mellow Cotswold stone. The museum's displays focus on 19th and early 20th century social, domestic and agricultural activities, whilst one fascinating exhibition documents the life story of a local farm-labourer, John Hodges of Butleigh, from cradle to grave. Choose the right day (telephone Glastonbury 32903) and you could also see practical demonstrations of traditional local crafts such as butter- or cider-making, or even a display by a group of local Morris Dancers.

Cheddar and the Gorge

Introduction: The true grandeur of the Mendip Hills can only be fully appreciated when approached from the south across the Somerset Levels. The limestone mass of the Mendips, stretching for some 30 miles across the northern boundary of Somerset, rises to a height of 1,067 feet above sea-level at Blackdown, a lonely hilltop high above Burrington Combe. Without doubt, the most spectacular surface feature on Mendip is Cheddar Gorge, whose vertical cliffs rise to a height of almost 500 feet. This walk explores parts of the area normally unseen by visitors and the highlight is assuredly the cliff-top path that runs for almost 2 miles from Blackrock Gate back into Cheddar village. The views from the top of the cliffs are exhilarating, over such high spots as the Horseshoe Bend, the Pinnacles and Lion Rock. This is certainly the most dramatic inland rock scenery anywhere in Southern England.

Distance: This circular ramble around Cheddar and the Gorge covers a seemingly straightforward 5 miles. The only minor hiccup is the 650 feet climb out of Cheddar onto the Mendip Plateau that takes place within the first mile of the walk! Allow a comfortable 3 hours.

Refreshments: There are abundant refreshment facilities in Cheddar village, with perhaps a cream-tea sounding the most tempting alternative. Alongside the car-park is the *Butcher's Arms* public-house.

How to get there: Cheddar lies just off the A371 Wells to Axbridge road. A short distance north of the A371, on the

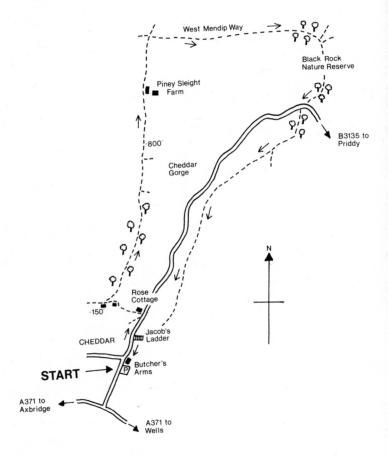

'B' class road that leads up into the gorge, you will find the *Butcher's Arms* public house on the right-hand side. Alongside the pub, there is a local authority car-park. (GR 461537)

The Walk: Leave the car-park, turn right and follow the road up through the lower end of Cheddar Gorge. Pass the gift shops, the cider stores, the chip bars, the crazy golf, and the crazy everything else! A few hundred yards beyond

Jacob's Ladder, you will find Rose Cottage on the left-hand side, just beyond the top end of the Water Board's reservoir. Immediately in front of Rose Cottage, turn left onto an unmetalled track that gradually begins to climb the Mendip foothills. Upwards we proceed!

It is not long before open views appear to the left, across Cheddar and the neighbouring market-gardens. In July, the air is thick with the aroma of strawberries. Shortly, in front of a driveway leading to a house, the path bears right to pass behind a cottage. The path brings you out behind another dwelling. Here, follow the path that slopes back up the hill to the right.

For ½ mile the route is obvious, ever-onwards, ever-upwards, climbing the wooded western slopes of Cheddar Gorge. The only consolation is the abundance of shade! Where the woodland begins to thin out, the path passes over a stile on the left-hand side. The gradient is by now much less severe. Beyond the stile, the path bears to the right to follow the right-hand field boundary – an overgrown, tumbledown wall – on up the hillside for a further ½ mile.

Ignore all gateways and signposted paths to the right, continuing straight on until eventually, just beyond an area of scrubland, you reach the open Mendip plateau, over 800 feet above sea level, and a flagstone stile with an iron bar on top. The view to the south from this stile is especially fine. From left to right can be seen Glastonbury Tor, the surrounding Levels, Cheddar Gorge, Brent Knoll, and the Bristol Channel, all against a backdrop of the Blackdown Hills, the Quantocks, and distant Exmoor.

Beyond the stile, the path follows the left-hand field boundary across three fields until Piney Sleight Farm is reached. Pass to the left of the farmhouse – yes, through the garden and in front of the back-door! – and follow the enclosed farm drive for some 300 yards until a stile and a signpost on the right-hand side point you in the direction of Cheddar via the West Mendip Way.

Follow the right-hand field boundary for well over ½ mile

until a stile takes you into Long Wood, and you proceed downhill through a delightful aisle of hazel trees. You emerge from the trees at the northern end of the Black Rock Nature Reserve, a magnificent dry limestone valley with many fine rock exposures. This is a truly delightful spot.

Continue to the right down through the reserve, ignoring two stiles early on to the left – the first into Long Wood Nature Reserve, the second into the delightfully named Velvet Bottom. Black Rock Nature Reserve is an all too brief ½ mile of pure beauty, and soon you will reach the B3135 Cheddar to Priddy road – but never mind, even better scenery is in store.

Cross the B3135, climb the stile almost directly opposite, and a short, sharp ascent through the trees brings you to the high ground at the top end of Cheddar Gorge. Having secured the open ground above the woodland, follow the well-worn path towards Cheddar. Shortly, there is a left-hand fork to Draycott, which you ignore, beyond which the path follows the cliff top, many hundreds of feet above the road.

Across the Gorge, the path that you took out of Cheddar earlier in the day can be seen, and perhaps even the metal-barred stile where perhaps you rested. The scenery is sublime, and almost defies human description. It is certainly worth pointing out the danger facing you if you decide to creep near the cliff edge to view the matchbox cars and coaches many hundreds of feet below!

Eventually, the path brings you to the top of Jacob's Ladder and Prospect Tower. Descend the 300 or so steps of the ladder back down to the road, turn left, and within a few hundred yards you will find the *Butcher's Arms* and the car-park where the walk began.

Historical Notes

Cheddar is, of course, home to one of the world's famous cheeses. The town is also noted as a strawberry-growing centre, sited ideally beneath the sheltered south-facing slopes of the Mendip Hills, although foreign competition is threatening this industry. Other places of interest are the town's Medieval Market Cross, the 14th century church of St Andrew and the schoolhouse where Hannah More started her philanthropic work. However, most visitors to Cheddar come for just two reasons – the caves and the gorge.

The gorge was carved out by running water in a bygone era. Rainwater contains a mild solution of acid, which readily dissolves the cracks and joints found in the Mendip limestone. The same process explains the many caves and caverns that honeycomb the local subterranean landscape. The running water is still there, but only the pot-holers can testify to its existence. The gorge is truly impressive, especially when approached from Priddy – vast, sheer limestone cliffs, up to 500 feet in height, dotted with squat yew trees and whitebeam, the rare alpine pennygrass and the Cheddar pink. The rock ledges provide nesting grounds for the many jackdaws whose squawks echo constantly around the gorge. The two main cave systems open to the public are Cox's and Gough's. George Cox discovered his collection of underground passages in the 1830s, and contained within are spectacular stalagmite pillars and stalactite curtains, together with strange rock formations with equally strange names such as 'Mermaid and Mummy' and 'Lady Chapel'. Gough's was discovered in the 1890s, although the bones and primitive tools contained within dated back to palaeolithic man. The 12,000 year old skeleton of what has been referred to as 'Cheddar man' was found in Gough's in 1903, and is exhibited today in the cave's museum. Jacob's Ladder, a flight of over 300 steps, climbs the cliff face at the lower end of the gorge to reach Prospect Tower. From the tower, fine views of the gorge, the Mendip Hills, the Somerset Levels and the distant Quantock Hills can be enjoyed.

The West Mendip Way was devised and waymarked by the

Rotary Clubs of Weston-super-Mare, Wrington Vale, Mendip and Wells to commemorate the Queen's Silver Jubilee in 1977. It runs from Uphill on the coast just south of Weston, through to the delightful cathedral city of Wells, a distance of some 30 miles along the ridge of the Mendip Hills. A couple of days spent exploring the West Mendip Way provides a perfect introduction to the delights of the area, for the places along the route read like a 'Who's Who' of the Mendip landscape – Wookey Hole, Ebbor Gorge, Priddy, Cheddar Gorge, Shipham and Crook Peak. *The West Mendip Way – The Walker's Guide* by Derek Moyes is the perfect companion to the route, and is available in most bookstores locally.

The Black Rock Nature Reserve at the head of Cheddar Gorge consists of 183 acres of rough grassland, plantation, natural woodland and scree, all sited in and around a dry limestone valley. Within the reserve lies the former Black Rock Quarry, with clearly exposed sections of limestone. It is easy to spot the vertical cracks or 'joints' in the rock through which the rainwater drains away very quickly. This results in a dry valley, with the rivers and streams deep underground flowing through elaborate cave and tunnel systems. Alongside the former workings is an old lime-kiln. Lime was produced by heating the limestone rock from the quarry with coal or charcoal. The lime was then used either in mortar for strengthening walls, or it was spread on the fields of the Mendip plateau where leaching by heavy rainfall removes the natural lime from the soil. Informative leaflets are available at the reserve that describe its varied flora and fauna.

Brean Down

Introduction: The bold limestone headland of Brean Down juts out into the sea, separating Avon's Weston-super-Mare from the smaller resorts of Somerset. From its summit, 320 feet above sea-level, it is possible to do a visual tour of much of Somerset. To the east lie the Mendip Hills – and how easy it is to see that Brean is simply a western outlier of this hill range; the Somerset Levels, dominated by Glastonbury Tor and Brent Knoll, are spread out to the south and south-east; the uplands of Exmoor and the Quantocks lie south and south-west, whilst closer at hand is the vast sweep of Bridgwater Bay. It is not difficult to see why Brean Down has been a favoured location for defensive fortifications down through the centuries, most recently, during the Second World War as an anti-aircraft unit. The Down is far more peaceful today, with its exceptional natural history making it is a Site of Special Scientific Interest.

Distance: A short circuit of just 3 miles, that will easily fill a leisurely couple of hours.

Refreshments: Alongside the car-park is a beach cafe that serves a range of snacks.

How to get there: Burnham-on-Sea lies just 2 miles west of junction 22 on the M5. From Burnham, follow the coast road northwards through Berrow and Brean until the road ends just below Brean Down. There is a car-park here alongside the beach-shop. (GR 296585)

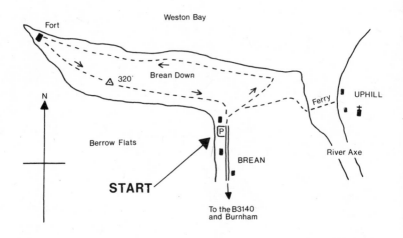

The Walk: Route-finding around Brean Down is a simple matter indeed. There is but one circuit around the headland, and a wrong turn would either leave you ploughing through a dense undergrowth of bracken or plunging into the murky waters of the Bristol Channel! Nevertheless, there is a need for a few simple directions.

Leave the car-park and continue along the lane signposted 'To the Ferry'. You will very shortly pass the Tropical Bird Gardens on your left. Do not climb the daunting flight of steps onto Brean Down, but carry on for a short distance to a path on the left that makes the ascent more gradually. At the top of this path is an information board, and wide-ranging views northwards of Weston Bay.

Continue onto the western end of the Down, along the lower path that keeps to the Weston side of the hill. Eventually, you will reach the remains of the 19th century fort, where undoubtedly you will pause to explore what remains of this part of the Bristol Channel defences. From the fort, follow the path that climbs the ridge towards the summit of Brean Down and its triangulation pillar, where views southwards across Berrow Flats open up.

Continue along the undulating ridge back inland, until immediately above the car-park you will find yourself at the top of the steep flight of steps mentioned earlier. It is now your privilege to make the remaining short steep descent back to the car-park where the walk began, smiling sympathetically at the walkers with the daunting prospect of climbing the stairway!

Historical Notes

Brean Down, a western outlier of the Mendip Hills, is formed of carboniferous limestone laid down in a shallow sea 300 million years ago. The rock was formed from the remains of marine animals, chiefly shellfish and coral, whose fossilized remains can still be found around the Down. Rock folding, some 30 million years later, gave the headland its distinctive shape. Today, due to its outstanding coastal habitats, Brean Down is a scheduled Site of Special Scientific Interest. The steeper south-facing slopes house jackdaws, kestrels and rock pipits on their rocky ledges, whilst the north side of the ridge slopes gradually to Weston Bay with its mudflats, salt-marsh and wading birds. Peak migration times bring thousands of birds to the area.

Brean has a long and varied history of settlement. At its eastern end lie the remains of an Iron Age hillfort (such a useful strategic site that during the Second World War it was used for gun emplacements). These Iron Age settlers were in all probability not the valiant men-of-war that the term 'fort' implies, with farming being their main occupation. Around the east and west knolls of the Down, the low banks running across the line of the footpath are the relics of their field systems. Although the Romans arrived in Britain in AD 43, and were not long in discovering the lead deposits underlying Mendip, establishing a small exporting port across the Axe at either Uphill or Bleadon, it was not until AD 340 that the Romans arrived on Brean and constructed a Temple. Local quarried stone was used in its construction, together with Bath stone for the archways and pennant slates from Bristol for the roofing. The Temple was only used for worship for 30 years before falling into ruin. Information boards around Brean give details of both sites, including their precise locations.

The next major developments on the Down occurred in the 19th century. 1861 saw the formation of the Brean Down Harbour Company. The Company planned a major port installation at the seaward end of Brean, with a direct rail-link to the nearby Bristol and Exeter railway, to offer amongst other attractions a faster transatlantic passenger service than that being offered out of Liverpool. On 5th November, 1864, there were great celebrations as local dignitaries took a paddle-steamer from Weston to Brean, accompanied by the Town Band and backed by the sound of a gun salute, to lay the foundation stone of the harbour. That night, perhaps as an omen, the foundation stone was washed out to sea and later recovered close to Steep Holm! Work continued sporadically on the project, but was eventually abandoned.

Around the same time, the expansion of French military strength under Napoleon III, including the development of the first iron-clad battleship *La Gloire*, caused Lord Palmerston to establish a Royal Commission to investigate the 'Defences of the United Kingdom'. From this 1859 Commission, a series of sea defences resulted including those along the Bristol Channel. Forts were established at Brean Down, Steep Holm, Flat Holm and Lavernock Point in South Wales to defend the ports at Cardiff, Newport and Bristol. The Brean site was equipped with seven 7-inch rifled muzzle-loading cannon, and manned by the Coast Brigade, Royal Artillery.

Only two moments of real excitement occurred for the Artillery during their stay on Brean. In 1896, Marconi sent his first over-the-water wireless message from Brean to Steep Holm, whilst on 6th July 1900, Gunner Haines fired his carbine down the shaft of a ventilator into number 3 magazine, beneath the western gun positions. He succeeded in killing himself and virtually destroyed the fort in the process! The complex was closed, the guns were hauled away by traction engine, and until 1939 the site operated as a cafe. There was one further spell of action when the fort was rearmed with two 6-inch naval guns and two searchlight batteries during the Second World War, and manned by 571 Regiment Coast Artillery, Western Command.

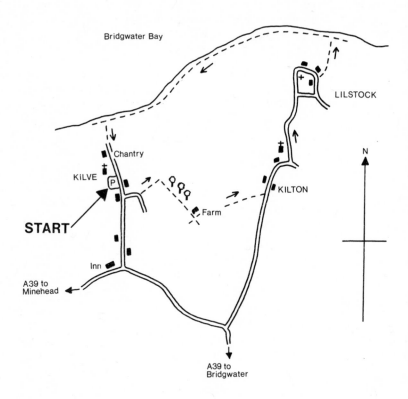

Bridgwater Bay

LILSTOCK

Chantry

KILVE

P

START

KILTON

Farm

Inn

A39 to
Minehead

A39 to
Bridgwater

N

Kilve and Bridgwater Bay

Introduction: Few travellers heading across West Somerset venture north of the main Minehead road to explore the coastline east of Watchet. This is an intriguing landscape with clifftop paths, crumbling rock faces, pebbly beaches and more than a little sense of history. The local shale is oil-bearing, and Kilve had aspirations in the 1920s to become the Dallas of Somerset. In earlier times, there was a chantry in the village, and to this day its ivy-clad ruins adorn the roadside just below the church. It was destroyed by fire in 1850, and the emerald and blue colouration of the flames confirmed local suspicions that here was a hot-bed of liquor smuggling. The oil magnates and the smugglers have long since gone, leaving a peaceful corner of Somerset for today's walker to explore and enjoy.

Distance: The ramble covers a distance of just over 5 miles. It can be comfortably completed in 2½ or 3 hours.

Refreshments: There are no refreshment facilities on the actual route. On the main A39 at the southern end of Kilve, just over ½ mile from the start of the walk, the *Hood Arms* serves liquid refreshment as well as a range of meals and snacks.

How to get there: Kilve lies on the A39 Minehead to Bridgwater road, 5 miles east of Williton. Follow the lane that leads to the coast from the main road, and park carefully alongside St Mary the Virgin church. (GR 147439)

The Walk: With your back to the churchyard gate at Kilve, head up Sea Lane, in the direction of the main road, and turn left opposite Meadow House. This lane climbs a slight rise, and where it bears to the right, continue straight ahead onto an enclosed track. At the end of this track, climb the gate and follow the footpath signposted to the right, a concrete bridge crossing the small stream alongside the stile.

Beyond the stile, follow a path through three fields to Lower Hill Farm, which is derelict and in ruins. In the first two fields, the path borders the woodland to the left, before crossing a paddock to emerge onto a crosstrack to the right of the farm.

Ignore a signposted track and stile immediately ahead, instead turning left to pass in front of the ruined farmhouse to reach a gateway. The path beyond the gate passes through two open arable fields, keeping the hedgerow immediately to the right, before crossing a smaller third field to emerge onto a lane just to the south of Kilton. This open countryside east of Lower Hill Farm provides the first real views of Bridgwater Bay, with Hinkley Point, Steep Holm and the more distant Welsh coast being especially prominent.

Turn left at the lane, and pass down through the complex of farm-buildings either side of the road that make up West Kilton and East Kilton Farms (not derelict!) Continue through Kilton until you reach the marvellously isolated church of St Nicholas, a red-sandstone building whose colouration makes it especially prominent for many miles around.

Continue northwards along the quiet country lanes to reach Lilstock. (It is worth hunting out the derelict church of St Andrew, along a grassed track on the right-hand side as you enter the hamlet). Continue on through Lilstock, the road bearing to the right and dropping downhill to reach Lilstock Farm. Just beyond the farm, turn left and follow the pot-holed track that heads north to the coast. It is actually signposted as leading to the beach parking area.

The 2 or 3 miles back to Kilve are simple to find. All you

need do is turn left at the coastal-path and continue westwards. The clifftop is unfenced, and there are steep drops in several places, so please keep a careful eye on your youngsters – and miscreant grown-ups!

Eventually the path drops down to Kilve Pill, where you turn left alongside the freshwater pool to head inland towards Kilve. You will pass two interesting ruins: the first represents the remains of the local oil retort house, whilst the second is the ivy-clad walls of a 14th century Chantry. Follow the lane to return to the church where the walk began.

Historical Notes

Kilve Chantry, a modest establishment for just five priests, was founded in 1329 by Sir Simon de Furneaux. Its dissolution occurred long before Henry VIII inflicted his reign of terror on monastic establishments, speculation suggesting that the heretical Sir Richard Stury – who had married into the Furneaux Estate – wished to see his wife's spending directed elsewhere! Subsequently, local farmers saw the chantry as ideal for hay storage, whilst cattle would shelter within its confines during storms. Later still, the chantry acted as a store for contraband, with brandy kegs being hidden in the pool on Kilve beach before being retrieved and carried inland. It was only when a local carter became so inebriated on neat spirits he dropped down dead that a local magistrate became suspicious and ordered an investigation. Mysteriously, the chantry caught alight one dark night in 1850 before the investigations had begun, and the emerald and blue flames subtly hinted that the contents were somewhat more than just hay! Such a chequered history behind what is today simply an ivy-clad ruin.

The Shaline Company was established in 1924 with the aim of 'developing an important industry in Somerset' – the industry in question being oil-extraction. Kilve was to be operational headquarters. The project followed the discovery in 1916 of oil shales, 1,000 feet deep and extending for over 8,000 acres between Watchet and the Parret estuary. The shale continued inland for as much as 2 miles, and was estimated to contain perhaps 5 million gallons of oil. The dreams of a Somerset 'Texas' were unfulfilled, however, due to the high production costs of the enterprise, vast quantities of shale waste being generated in the production of quite small amounts of oil. The oil retort house, a red-brick construction dating from the mid 1920s, stands at Kilve as testimony to this fascinating episode in the village's history. Crushed shale would have been loaded into a cast-iron cylindrical structure at the top of the retort house, and then subjected to great heat. The gaseous substance that was produced by this process was condensed to form a liquid roughly akin to crude oil.

St Nicholas Church, Kilton, received but a scanty note in Pevsner's *Buildings of England*: 'St Nicholas 1862 by John Norton incorporating Perp. bits.' In fact, the building is a great deal older than the 19th century, the 'Perp. bits' being virtually just the chancel arch and the lower tower, both dating from the 14th century. In 1862 the church was extensively restored by the Victorian architect John Norton, when the top stage of the tower was added, and some of the chancel windows were replaced by lancets. The church is plain and functional, with perhaps little to catch the eye of the architectural purist, but its beauty lies in its pure simplicity. There is little by way of stained glass, carvings or monuments, the only notable decorations being the Victorian Biblical texts that are painted around the church. Over the vestry door there appears a timely reminder for the officiating minister that 'thy priests be clothed with righteousness'. It is a pity that such a warning was not more prominent in 1554 when the vicar was reported as a 'common sower of discord and dissension among his parishioners and a common slanderer of them'. He had given nothing to the church, had spent nothing at the Church Ale, and had preached nothing from the pulpit for three or four years!

Glatting was an activity widely practised along the foreshore at Kilve in centuries past. The word 'glat' was the local name for the conger eel, examples of which up to 10 feet in length and with the most vicious of teeth, can be found under the rocks amongst the grey mud. When there were exceptionally low tides, hunts would be organised into the eels' hiding places. Terriers and spaniels would be trained as 'fish-hounds' to accompany teams of men armed with heavy clubs. The 'field' would plunge into the mud, and lever up the rocks in the hope of striking it lucky. Just occasionally, the mud would fly, furious flashing teeth would be sighted and a catch would be taken. The sport is now rarely prac-tised – I wonder why?

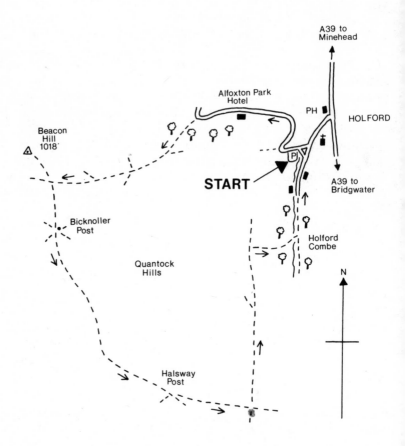

A39 to Minehead

HOLFORD

PH

A39 to Bridgwater

Alfoxton Park Hotel

START

Beacon Hill 1018'

Bicknoller Post

Quantock Hills

Holford Combe

Halsway Post

N

Wordsworth's Quantocks: Holford and Alfoxton House

Introduction: It is little wonder that Samuel Taylor Coleridge settled at Nether Stowey, to be followed by William Wordsworth at nearby Holford, for these great English poets instantly recognised the beauty of the neighbouring Quantock Hills. This is a fine landscape of wooded combes, open moorland, ridge-paths and streams, where even the most soulless would surely find inspiration. Dorothy Wordsworth summed up the Quantocks in a very economical phrase:

'Their great beauty is their wild simplicity'.

Distance: This circular ramble covers some 6 miles, and can be comfortably completed in 2½ to 3 hours.

Refreshments: On the A39 Minehead to Bridgwater road, ½ mile from the end of the walk, the *Plough Inn* offers full meals or snacks. Opposite the Inn is the Chestnut Tree Tea Rooms.

How to get there: Holford lies on the A39 Bridgwater to Minehead road, 6 miles east of Williton. Turn off the main road at the *Plough Inn*, follow the winding lane through the village until a little way beyond the church you reach a fork. Bear right, signposted 'Alfoxton and Hodder's Combe', to reach Holford Green where there is ample space for parking. (GR 154411)

The Walk: Leave the parking area, and continue westwards along the lane out of Holford. The lane bends to the right alongside the old village dog pound; continue along this route signposted to the *Alfoxton Park Hotel*. It is little more than ½ mile to the hotel, an 18th century manor house where Wordsworth lived for one year in 1797.

Continue along the lane beyond the hotel, as it begins to climb up onto the Quantocks. Where the lane bears to the right, a short distance up from the hotel, continue straight on following a footpath into the woods. It is not too long before you emerge onto the open moorland, where a sign-post marks the spot where several paths converge. Continue to climb directly up the hillside, following the route sign-posted to 'West Quantoxhead and Staple Plain'.

At the next junction, continue straight on, ignoring the left turn signposted to 'Bicknoller Post' – you are to follow a slightly different course to reach this sturdy wooden stake. Fork left at the next junction, and continue on to a cross-roads where the ridge-top path crosses the Holford to East Quantoxhead track that you have been following. Beacon Hill, 1,018 feet above sea-level, is clearly visible to the right, and well worth a detour. The crossroads is blessed with a marker-post, where you turn left to head due south along the Quantock Ridge.

Bicknoller Post is passed on the left in a few hundred yards, a landmark upon which so many tracks converge that the spot looks like an asterisk on the OS map! Continue along the ridge path, passing to the right of the stake, 100 yards beyond which you should fork to the left to continue along the main track. The views are far-ranging wherever you look, with few trees around what is essentially a bracken- and heather-clad hilltop.

The path continues on ahead, twisting and occasionally climbing, until in a mile or so you reach the point shown on the 1:25 000 map as Halsway Post, although this time there is no sign of a sturdy wooden post. The approach to Halsway Post is heralded by a small white gas pipeline marker-stone on the right-hand side, and a pair of fire-beaters to the left of the ridge-path.

At this junction of many paths, turn left along a double track that skirts the side of the hill, the land dropping away steeply to Stert and Somerton Combes below. In about ½ mile, you will reach a fairly prominent crossroads, where you turn left to follow the ridge that separates Somerton Combe to the west from Holford Combe to the east. The path is clear and distinct, and at the first junction bear right to drop steadily downhill, the left fork climbing to Higher Hare Knap. Within a few hundred yards, turn right to follow the grass path down through the bracken to reach Holford Combe.

In the combe, pass through a marshy woodland area before fording the actual stream. On its far bank, turn left to follow the track back to Holford. The track eventually becomes a lane, the *Combe House Hotel* is passed on the left-hand side, and then a variety of attractive cottages follow. Turn left past the pillar-box, then sharp left to arrive back at Holford Green and the parking area, where the walk began.

Historical Notes

Alfoxton House was home to the poet William Wordsworth and his sister Dorothy during 1797, their move west being prompted by the desire to maintain a friendship with Samuel Taylor Coleridge. Coleridge was at this time living in nearby Nether Stowey, in a cottage that is today a National Trust property. Alfoxton was a good deal smaller in 1797 than the hotel that occupies the site today, the side wings not having been added until 1805. The winding drive leads to what can best be described as a solid and sober house rather than a glorious mansion. The group of friends took regular excursions onto the Quantocks, walking the hills in all weathers, admiring the distant sea-views and exploring the wooded combes. It was a particularly productive spell, with Coleridge inspired to write such pieces as *The Ancient Mariner* and *Kubla Khan* whilst the joint collection of *Lyrical Ballads* was inevitably inspired by this glorious corner of Somerset. It is fitting to quote from the journals of Dorothy Wordsworth:

> 'Wherever we turn we have woods, smooth downs and valleys with small brooks running down them through meadows hardly ever intersected with hedgerows but scattered over with trees. The Hills that cradle these villages are either covered with fern or bilberries or oakwoods – walks extended for miles over the hilltops, the great beauty of which is their wild simplicity'.

It may seem strange that the Wordsworths, given their attachment to the Quantock Hills, should have stayed for such a short period of time. In fact, they had no choice! After just a year, the owner of Alfoxton refused to renew their tenancy. It was the time of the French Revolution, and the poet's sympathy with the cause together with his mystifying habit of taking lengthy strolls under cover of darkness, led to suspicions that he was a French spy.

Holford Dog Pound, sited at the entrance to Alfoxton's driveway, has an interesting history that inspired Wordsworth's poem *Simon Lee*. The local fox-hounds were kept in kennels at the top of the deer-park behind Alfoxton. It was the normal practice to store the dogs' meat by hanging it from the branches of nearby trees. Of course, this attracted all the stray dogs of the neighbourhood who would collect under the 'pantry trees' howling with hunger and snapping at the meat. Naturally, the commotion would trigger off the fox-hounds! On one especially noisy night, Christopher Tricky, the huntsman, dressed hurriedly and ran off to try and put a stop to the uproar. In his haste, he forgot to don his huntsman's coat, the sight and smell of which told the dogs that here was their master. The unknowing hounds proceeded to tear him to pieces! To prevent a recurrence of this sad event, a dog pound was built at the entrance to the drive to house the village strays.

Holford, the name, derives from the settlement's geographical location. The village lies in a combe – or hole – where the original coach road dipped down and forded the local stream. The road, known locally as Stowey Road, crossed the water near the village's thatched cottages, before passing Holford Green and climbing Dog Pound Lane onto Longstone Hill. Between the car-park and the dog pound, we are effectively following this route. In the 16th century, Huguenot exiles settled in the village and established a silk factory at the head of the glen, the soft Quantock water being excellent for the dyeing process. When the French Revolution blocked the import of raw silk, the factory switched to blanket-making. The whole exercise ended abruptly in 1820 when a major fire destroyed the factory. During the 19th century a local man, James Hayman, established a tannery where the *Combe House Hotel* stands today. As you pass the hotel towards the end of the ramble, you will see the fine waterwheel in the grounds that was used as a power source in the tanning process, which involved local bark and valonia from Asia Minor. The most noted feature of St Mary's church is to be found in the graveyard – the resting place of Frederick Norton, whose musical, *Chu-Chin-Chow*, had a London run of 2,238 consecutive appearances. Architecturally, the church has a rather short west tower and a saddleback roof. It was largely rebuilt in the mid 19th century.

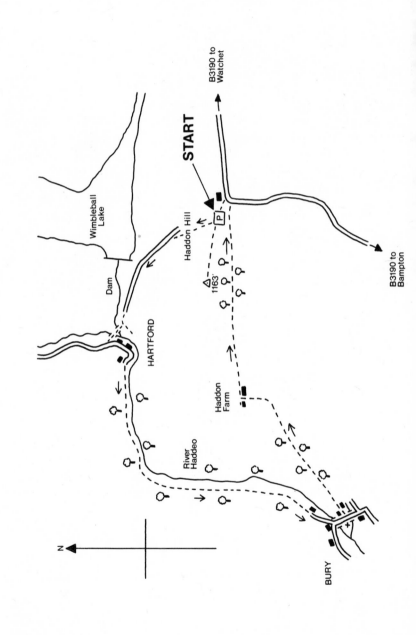

Haddon Hill and Wimbleball Lake

Introduction: East of Dulverton, in the extreme south-eastern corner of the Exmoor National Park, lies the lovely Haddeo Valley. The valley contains one of those delightful Exmoor rivers whose shallow waters tumble and splash across a rock-strewn bed. Above the valley lies Haddon Hill, an area of fine unspoiled heather moorland. Surprisingly, it is a man-made feature that provides the 'icing-on-the-cake' for this ramble in the form of Wimbleball Lake. This vast reservoir occupies the centre of the Haddeo Valley, and its beauty is undoubted compensation for the loss of wilderness that occurred in the 1970s when the area was flooded. A ramble that could rightly be subtitled 'Far from the madding crowd'.

Distance: A circuit of some 5½ miles that will comfortably fill some 2½ to 3 hours.

Refreshments: There are no refreshment facilities on or near the route. The weary traveller will have to drive 5 miles south from the picnic and parking area to reach Bampton, over the border in Devon, where local cream teas are a speciality.

How to get there: The parking area on Haddon Hill lies alongside the B3190 Watchet to Bampton road. Leave the road at the right-angle bend 1½ miles west of Upton, cross the cattle-grid and follow the signs to the car-park. (GR 969285)

The Walk: The northern side of the car-park provides fine views down to Wimbleball Lake. There is a stile in the fence here, beyond which you should follow the path down the hillside signposted 'Dam ¾'. Very shortly, turn left along the Water Board's access road and continue downhill to the dam, tinged in a touching shade of pink to blend in with the local landscape! The ramble continues straight ahead following the path signposted to 'Hartford'.

The path continues downhill, the waters of the Haddeo in the dip to the right. At a fork a little way beyond a cattle-grid bear right and follow the path signposted 'Bury – avoiding houses' which brings you onto a country lane. Turn left and pass through the tiny hamlet of Hartford, with the Mill to the left and the Lodge to the right and precious little else besides!

Beyond the Lodge the lane ends, and continuing beyond the gateway is a riverside path that you follow for a delightful 2 or 3 miles to Bury. This is fine walking – on either side are steep wooded valley sides, whilst to the left tumble the sparkling waters of the Haddeo across their rocky bed. Eventually the path ends and you join a lane that leads into Bury, a village of attractive cottages grouped around a packhorse bridge and a ford across the Haddeo. This is probably a good place to pause and enjoy that flask of coffee in the rucksack!

Turn left at the junction alongside the Old Schoolhouse, cross the river and continue along the road until you come to a converted Methodist chapel on the right-hand side. Almost opposite, a cul-de-sac lane leads up through a collection of cottages, with names to match the atmosphere hereabouts – Pixton Barn, Rockspray and Virginia Cottage. Directly ahead, half-hidden in summer months by grass and nettles, is a gate, which leads onto a sunken tree-lined track, very rocky underfoot, and running with water following heavy rainfall. (Ignore a more obvious gateway to the right alongside the cottages.)

Follow the track uphill for close on ½ mile until at the

hilltop it passes through a magnificent wooded glade before becoming a wide grass path bound by hedgerows. This really is one of the most marvellously secretive paths that I have been fortunate enough to stumble across, seemingly little-used, a true relic from the era when footpaths were the roads of their day carrying people and animals from farmhouses to churches, from hilltops to valleys.

The path bears to the left and continues, still enclosed and increasingly overgrown, on to Haddon Farm. In summer months, it may be necessary to use the adjoining fields in the final approach to the Farm, with the path perhaps hidden beneath a sea of nettles.

At Haddon Farm, over 900 feet above sea-level, turn right and follow the track back to the B3190. You come out on the right-angled bend noted in the 'How to get there' section. To your left is the track leading into the car-park where the walk began.

Although officially the end of the ramble, it is worth walking the ½ mile to the triangulation pillar atop Haddon Hill to enjoy the views that clockwise, starting from the north-east, read the Quantocks, the Wellington Monument and the Blackdown Hills, Yes Tor and Dartmoor, Winsford Hill and Dunkery Beacon. With no refreshment facilities on the walk, why not pack a picnic to enjoy on Haddon Hill as the perfect end to a fine Somerset Ramble?

Historical Notes

Wimbleball Lake is the largest reservoir on Exmoor, extending over an area of 370 acres and with a capacity of 4,250 million gallons. Construction of the dam across the Haddeo Valley took place between November 1974 and December 1977, when filling commenced. In an area like Exmoor, there were concerns and fears for the environmental damage that the project might cause, but careful landscaping based upon plans drawn up by Dame Sylvia Crowe has produced what is an asset for the National Park. To allay environmental concerns, the 160 foot high dam was even tinged pink to match the local stone! The reservoir supplies towns from Bridgwater and Taunton down to Tiverton and Exeter with their water, as well as being a major recreational amenity. There is fine fly-fishing on Wimbleball, for example, with an annual restocking of over 20,000 rainbow trout occurring. The record catch to date has been an 8½ pound specimen.

The River Haddeo rises on the Brendon Hills, before flowing through Wimbleball Reservoir to join the river Exe a mile south of Bury. The name Haddeo has an interesting derivation – 'had' is probably a corruption of 'head' whilst the suffix 'eo' is derived from the Anglo-Saxon for 'running water'. What we have as a consequence is a name that rather aptly means 'chief running water'. The pathway that follows the Haddeo between Hartford and Bury is a part of Lady Harriet's Drive, named after Lady Harriet Acland who planned the bridleway in about 1800. Today it is the stalking naturalists rather than the carriaged-gentry that are likely to be encountered along the river-bank. The thick woodland that borders the Haddeo harbours red deer, and provides an opportunity to observe the trees of a mixed woodland: oak, birch, beech, hazel and rowan. In April and May the woodland floor is a carpet of bluebells, whilst ornithologists may care to note that the oaks attract numbers of wood warblers as well as a few pairs of pied flycatchers.

Bury is a tiny hamlet tucked into the lower valley of the river Haddeo, a strange location for a settlement that literally means 'fortified place'. A glance at the OS map, however, explains all for there to the south-east of the village is Bury Castle. It is a motte-and-bailey construction on a hilltop overlooking the confluence of the Haddeo and the Exe. The 18th century historian Collinson wrote that it was a 'Roman work built on and inhabited by the Knightly family of Besilles'. The attractive village buildings are bisected by the river ford and a narrow packhorse bridge, not unlike the scene at Malmsmead or Allerford. The Old Schoolhouse, to the right as we enter Bury, was originally built as the village school in 1850. Forty years later it was replaced by a larger building and topped by a bell turret. Later still it served as an Anglican chapel, whilst today it stands as a private residence. Across the river we encounter a bastion of non-conformism, the slate-roofed Methodist chapel bearing the text 'Preach the Gospel to every Creature'. The message has apparently fallen on deaf ears for here, too, the former place of worship is a private residence. In the surrounding hillsides and woodlands, the daily bread was traditionally earned by charcoal-burning, and by slate and stone quarrying, whilst at Clammer – midway between Bury and Hartford – tin-mining was once attempted.

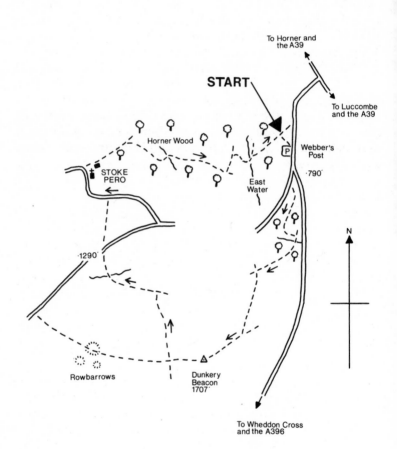

To Horner and
the A39

START

To Luccombe
and the A39

Horner Wood

STOKE
PERO

East
Water

Webber's
Post

·790·

·1290·

N

Rowbarrows

Dunkery
Beacon
1707·

To Wheddon Cross
and the A396

Stoke Pero and Dunkery Beacon

Introduction: Dunkery Beacon, at 1,707 feet, is not only the highest point in Somerset, it is also the highest point within the Exmoor National Park. In all directions, the eye feasts upon the sweeping moorland, the bare hilltops and the richly wooded combes, classic Exmoor landscape. With a sharp eye and a quiet disposition, you might well spot one of the red deer that frequent this wild part of Somerset. Hidden within one of the many combes is the tiny hamlet of Stoke Pero, with its tiny church that claims to be the highest, smallest and most remote on Exmoor. Certainly, the first claim is undeniably true. A strenuous ramble amidst a truly upland landscape where all of the basic ground-rules about appropriate footwear and clothing should be taken seriously.

Distance: A rugged 6½ miles that will easily fill somewhere between 3 and 4 hours.

Refreshments: There are no refreshment facilities on the walk itself. Wheddon Cross, a few miles south of Dunkery Beacon, is well-provided with the usual range of tourist amenities, including a tea-room that does a good line in delicious cream teas!

How to get there: From the A39 Minehead to Porlock road take either the Horner or Luccombe turnings. From either village, follow the signs for Dunkery Beacon until the road forks at Webber's Post for Cloutsham and Wheddon Cross.

Alongside the junction at Webber's Post is a large parking area. (GR 903438)

The Walk: Webber's Post provides fine views to the west of the oak woodland above Horner. A sign at the southern end of the car-park points the way, via the Cloutsham road, to the start of a nature trail. A short distance along the road, and this 'Woodland Trail' is signposted to the left. Follow the trail to marker stone number 2, which is found surrounded by oak trees alongside an attractive combe.

Avoid the temptation of crossing the stream at this point, rather take the path to the left that climbs steeply through a sea of whortleberry plants. Very soon, turn right at a junction to follow a well-used path through the stream, on through the woodland and out onto the open hillside.

Within ¼ mile a grassy track crosses your path. Turn left and follow this clear pathway onwards and upwards to the summit of Dunkery Beacon, passing around the head of a combe before forking to reach – at 1,707 feet – the highest point in Somerset. Dartmoor, the Welsh mountains, the Mendips, the Quantocks and Glastonbury Tor all fall within the encompass of the Beacon.

From the summit, head westwards in the general direction of Rowbarrows (consult the topograph on the summit if you have lost all sense of direction!) This hilltop path drops steadily until, within ¼ mile, it is crossed by a bridleway. Turn right and follow this path downhill for a little under one mile. All around is a fine moorland landscape, bare, open and exposed, home to the famous red deer of Exmoor.

At the foot of the hillside, turn left at a junction to follow the track signposted to Stoke Ridge. This path drops to cross the infant East Water before sweeping up the hillside to join the lane to Cloutsham. Follow the lane to the right, and in ½ mile turn left down another lane that leads to Stoke Pero church – a mile of road walking to reach the highest place of worship on Exmoor, 1,013 feet above sea-level.

Just beyond Church Farm, turn right to follow an enclosed

track that clips the corner of a field before entering an oak woodland. Almost immediately, you encounter a junction where the right-hand fork signposted to Webber's Post is taken.

Follow this path as it twists and turns through the woodland, dropping to cross the stream in Prickslade Combe at one point, until, within one mile, you emerge onto open ground. The car-park at Webber's Post is visible not too far ahead! A little way across the open ground is a seat facing due north towards Porlock Bay. This is point 5 of the nature trail, hence the marker stone.

Follow the path to the left at the junction below the seat, signposted as the 'Nature Trail', and turn right at the next junction to drop downhill to the now more-mature East Water. Turn left, cross the stream and Webber's Post is within shouting distance.

All that remains is a short – but sharp – ascent of some 300 feet up the path to the right. Within a few hundred yards, another path to the right through the native gorse returns you to the car-park where the walk began.

Historical Notes

Dunkery Beacon, 1,707 feet above the not too distant sea-level, is the highest point on Exmoor. This vast upland area is a plateau of ancient sandstone rocks which have been weathered and worn over millions of years by frosts, winds and rains. Its westerly location and high altitude mean that the moor has very high levels of rainfall, which runs off the impervious rocks to form fast-flowing streams. These have carved steep-sided valleys, or combes, for which Exmoor is so famous. High ground always has a long tradition of human habitation, and Dunkery Beacon and its environs proves no exception. The OS map reveals a proliferation of cairns, tumuli and barrows in the immediate area. The actual summit of Dunkery is strewn with the rough unhewn stones of ancient fire-hearths, and it is obviously as a 'beacon' in times of both danger and celebration that this lonely hilltop is best-known. The Armada was signalled from here on 19th July 1588, and 400 years later to the very day the hilltop was again ablaze in commemoration of this historical event. On the night of 6th June 1977, Dunkery Beacon linked similar beacons on the Quantocks and Mendip with a series of beacons in South Wales as a chain of fire spread throughout the Kingdom to celebrate the Queen's Silver Jubilee. Dunkery is much loved by naturalists, who roam the hillsides under cover of the autumn moon to hear the clashing of the stag 'bells' and who rise with the early morning sun to observe the majestic buzzard hovering overhead. It was, after all, Dunkery that provided the backdrop to Henry Williamson's tale of Stumberleap, the old stag. This is indeed a poetic place that 'rises in naked sublimity' and 'affords a noble prospect'.

Stoke Pero can rightly claim to possess the highest church on Exmoor, standing at 1,013 feet above sea-level, but St Peter's claim to also be the area's most remote and smallest place of worship would quite rightly be challenged by the parishioners of nearby Culbone. The first church on the site is thought to date from Celtic times, and would have been a small chapel used by a hermit. The Saxons endowed the hamlet with the name 'Stoke', meaning an 'enclosure or settlement', whilst the De Pirou family were granted the local land following the Norman Conquest. The name 'Stoke Pirou' is mentioned in the Domesday Book when the settlement consisted of the church and a small village. For centuries, this small community would have been self-supporting, the families working as hunters and farmers and collecting timber for fuel and building material. The parish appears to have faced difficulties attracting regular clergymen, probably due to its 'littleness and loneliness'. The church itself was totally restored by Sir Thomas Acland in 1897. Arthur Elliott-Cannon writing in the *Exmoor Review* of 1968 describes this most recent period of St Peter's history:

'We see not simply a restoration, but a new Church on an ancient site. Some mediaeval window frames have been incorporated, and old stones re-used; but there is little to remind us of the ancient building except a mediaeval door with door-posts cut from two enormous blocks of oak, and a font of indeterminate age ... The roof is rather splendid, with barrel-shaped oak beams, every fourth beam bearing a carved coat of arms or motif. All this timber was borne here by a Porlock donkey named Zulu, who padded his way twice a day from Parson Street, Porlock, to Stoke Pero, for many months in 1897. It seems fitting in this simple Church that Zulu should be commemorated, even if only with a framed notice.'

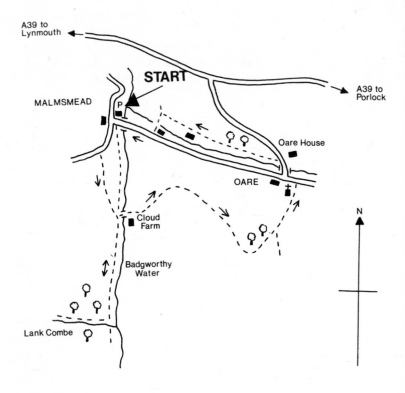

Lorna Doone Country: Oare and Malmsmead

Introduction: To lovers of English literature worldwide, the names Oare, Malmsmead and Badgworthy Water mean just one thing – Richard Blackmore's novel *Lorna Doone*. This classic tale, the story of Lorna's romance with John Ridd, is set against the violent activities of the marauding Doones. In this far corner of west Somerset, at times intruding into neighbouring Devon, we find a splendid Exmoor setting that acted as a backdrop to this classic piece of writing. The academic discussion that attempts to separate truth from fiction in this 19th century novel seems largely irrelevant as you walk through Doone Country. It is such an atmospheric location that one can almost sense Carver Doone lurking within the oak woodlands alongside the Badgworthy, or Lorna at the altar of Oare church, seconds before being gunned down. This is a ramble through the pages of a much-loved West Country legend.

Distance: A 5 mile ramble that should take no more than 2½ hours to complete. The section of the Doone Valley above Cloud Farm involves some retracing of our steps.

Refreshments: There are various tea-gardens in and around Malmsmead, whilst at Cloud Farm ploughman's lunches and cream teas can be purchased.

How to get there: Malmsmead lies along a network of narrow, winding lanes, where the passing-places tend to be well-used! To reach the village, turn off the A39 Porlock to

Lynmouth road, just a few hundred yards the Somerset side of County Gate. The turning is signposted to Oare. Having negotiated the hill down into the village, turn right at the junction by the church signposted to Malmsmead. Behind the gift-shop in Malmsmead, there is a large parking area and toilet facilities. (GR 792477)

The Walk: Ignore the 'short-cut' sign which involves paying a toll to cross private land and set off along the lane leading out of Malmsmead, signposted as leading to the 'Public Footpath to Doone Valley'. The lane climbs southwards out of the village, Badgworthy Water below to the left, until – where it bears to the right – you must continue along the waymarked path directly ahead. This leads to Cloud Farm, where you join the 'toll path' that has been following the riverbank from Malmsmead.

Without crossing the river continue southwards to explore deeper into the Doone Valley where the valley-sides steepen, the valley becomes narrower, the river-bed becomes rockier and the sound of the tumbling waters increases. This is actually beginning to feel like the rough and rugged terrain that a group of bandits like the Doones might inhabit! To many, this is 'the Doone Valley', but I wonder where the actual waterslide is that John Ridd struggled up to meet his beloved Lorna on a neighbouring grass sward?

If you continue along Badgworthy Water for close on one mile, beyond the Richard Blackmore memorial stone, the right-hand river-bank becomes heavily wooded. In the midst of this oak tree cover, a tributary stream joins the Badgworthy.

This is Lank Combe. At the top of the tumbling 'waterslide' here, there sits a grass sward, and one theory suggests that this is the entrance to the actual Doone Valley. The waterslide may look tame in mid-summer, but after winter rain it is a much more impressive sight.

After exploring Lank Combe return to Cloud Farm, retracing your steps along the Badgworthy. Below Cloud Farm a bridge crosses the river. The path beyond continues on to the farm buildings where you turn sharp left uphill on the path signposted to 'Oare Church'. This path climbs sharply up the hillside, before following vehicle tracks through to a wooded combe. Beyond the combe turn left to follow a grassy path down to Oare.

You will emerge to the right of the church that attracts thousands of visitors each year, most of whom come to stand and gaze at the spot where Lorna Doone met Carver's bullet on her wedding day. Across the valley stands Oare House, with Doone passages like 'Annie Ridd saw her father's funeral from the window of the house' suggesting to at least one researcher that here was the site of Plovers Barrows Farm.

From the church, cross the bridge over Oare Water, and in 100 yards turn left onto the path signposted to Malmsmead. The path passes through a spruce plantation, and goes to the right of Oaremead Farm before bearing left to cross a concrete arch bridge across the river. Continue up to Parsonage Farm, where a right-turn at the lane leads back to Malmsmead and the car-park where the walk began.

Historical Notes

Malmsmead is for most visitors the gateway to the Doone Valley. The tourists come to gaze at Lorna Doone Farm, where John Ridd is popularly believed to have brought his new wife, and to head south along the banks of Badgworthy Water to Lank Combe and Hoccombe, the very heart of Doone Country. The village has an idyllic setting – its white houses with their red-tiled roofs are grouped around the sparkling waters of the Badgworthy, where a traditional ford stands alongside a fine packhorse bridge. In the background are the white-washed stables, alive with the sound of hooves and voices. It is as picturesque as the photographs in the tourist guides suggest and it is therefore rather a 'honey-pot' for tourists.

Badgworthy Water, for the whole of its short existence of just 3 miles between Luccombe and Malmsmead, forms a natural boundary between Devon and Somerset. Below Malmsmead and the confluence with Oare Water, the two become East Lyn river. The Badgworthy with its tributaries and headwaters is traditionally accepted as Doone Country, with the actual location of the Doone Valley a matter of some debate. Sir Atholl Oakeley, in his booklet *The facts on which Blackmore based Lorna Doone*, comes down firmly on the side of Lank Combe, for it is only here that it is possible to scramble up a waterslide and find a grass sward at its summit. The original OS maps marked Hoccombe as the valley's location, whilst the current 1:50 000 plays safe by simply labelling Badgworthy Water as 'Doone Country'.

The Doones, incidentally, were more than simply fictional characters. Their notoriety was widespread in the district long before Blackmore's novel saw publication. They are thought to have been a group of Scots who came south in the 17th century, perhaps dispossessed Cavaliers or survivors of the Monmouth Rebellion. Before the publication of *Lorna Doone*, few people visited the Badgworthy and its only attraction was its fine trout fishing! A fascinating tale relates how Robert Gould, who hand-crafted his own flies, caught that many fish during one trip that he had to hire a horse-and-boy to return the catch to his home in Porlock! More recently, in the notorious winter of 1963, Farmer Bob Nancekivell at Cloud Farm was in desperate need of supplies of insulin. His son, Jim, had to use coal-dust to form the word 'Cloud' on the pure snow to direct the helicopter ferrying supplies to the district. Idyllic it may seem in mid-summer, but harsher the realities of life for the local population.

Oare attracts tens-of-thousands of visitors each year quite simply because of one passage in Blackmore's novel:

'The sound of a shot rang through the church, and those eyes were dim with death. Lorna fell across my knees . . . a flood of blood came out upon the yellow wood of the altar steps, and at my feet fell Lorna'.

Collinson, the parson-historian, described the countryside around Oare as 'very wild and romantick' and, fortunately, most visitors do take away with them more than simply the 'Doone experience'. Oare does not overplay its literary connections – even the church guidebook leaves mention of the altar incident to an almost incidental penultimate paragraph. The church of St Mary does indeed have a 'wild and romantick setting' – to quote Pevsner it lies 'in a green valley just behind a wall of hills'. The Perpendicular-style church contains delightful 18th century box-pews and pulpit, as well as a painting of Moses by Peter Spurrye, Churchwarden in 1718, a nicely-carved Prince of Wales feathers and the memorial to R D Blackmore. Blackmore's grandfather, incidentally, was once rector at the church.

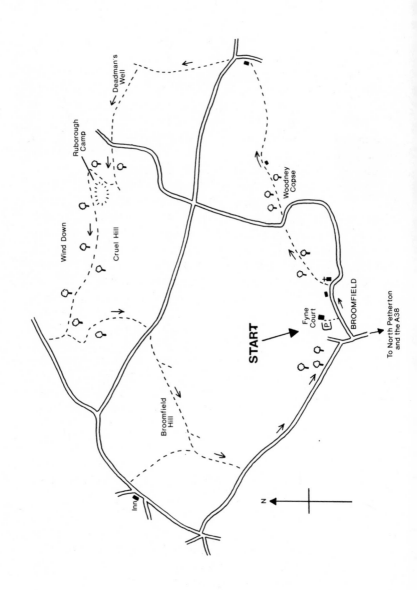

The Quantock Hills and Fyne Court

Introduction: Any visitor to the Quantock Hills should first visit Fyne Court in Broomfield, 6 miles north of Taunton. What remains of the home of Andrew Crosse, the Victorian electrical scientist, is now the headquarters of the Somerset Trust for Nature Conservation. As well as a gift shop, the centre contains displays and exhibits that illustrate the flora and fauna of this delightful hill-range. Above the Court rise the hills, perhaps less dramatic than further west where wooded combes and open moorland predominate, but no less beautiful for that. In and around Broomfield it was almost exclusively stock-rearing country until the 20th century. Today, however, dairy herds are common alongside the sturdy Red Devons and Dorset Horned sheep. Arable crops, chiefly barley and oats, have also been cultivated on these hills since wartime hostilities brought increased demands for food production. Views extend in all directions, encompassing Bridgwater Bay, the Mendip Hills, Sedgemoor and the Blackdowns.

Distance: A fairly strenuous 5½ miles, with names like Cruel Hill and Wind Down aptly describing sections of the route! Allow 3–3½ hours.

Refreshments: Teas can be bought at Fyne Court on Sundays and Bank Holidays during the summer. A short detour from the actual walk, shown on the map, will bring you to the *Traveller's Rest Inn*, high on Broomfield Hill.

WALK THIRTEEN

How to get there: Broomfield and Fyne Court lie 6 miles north of Taunton and 9 miles south-west of Bridgwater. Between these two towns on the A38 you will find North Petherton. From North Petherton, follow signposted lanes westwards to Broomfield. As you approach the village, the Court is well signposted. (GR 223322)

The Walk: The S.T.N.C. have waymarked this 5½ mile circuit. Look out for their symbol – a yellow '5' surrounded by a circle of arrows – as you follow the route.

From the car-park at Fyne Court, walk back down the driveway to the Broomfield road, turn left and shortly you will reach the village green and the adjoining church. It is well worth spending a few moments exploring 'Saint Mary and All Saints', if for no other reason than to see the richly carved bench ends dating from the 16th century and perhaps the most complete series in the country.

Turn left immediately before the churchyard to follow a path down through a combe, Roundabout Covert to the left, Churchman's Copse to the right. The path emerges onto the Broomfield to Enmore road, where you cross a stile directly opposite into Woodney Copse. The path climbs through the woodland onto open farmland, a tumbledown group of buildings ahead. This was a stockman's homestead until the Second World War, since when it has been abandoned.

Follow the path to the left of the ruin, which then continues across the top of the hillside to reach a lane in ¼ mile. There are fine views southwards all the while into a typical Quantock combe. Turn left at the lane, in front of a pair of houses, to reach a T-junction within 200 yards.

Turn left and, almost straight away, right onto a bridleway. Continue along the bridleway for a few hundred yards until it becomes a field-path. Continue downhill, with fine views ahead of Bridgwater and the Parrett Estuary, until half-way down the hillside a direction arrow points to your left. Here you follow the fence down into Deadman's Well. This ruined settlement is recorded in the Domesday Book, and traces of the cottage walls and gardens still remain. The path then climbs to emerge onto the Enmore road.

Cross over to enter the Forestry Commission's 'Wind Down'. Turn right at the first junction to begin the ascent of Cruel Hill. The name allegedly owes its origins to the fact that it represented a strenuous climb for horse-drawn vehicles in years gone by. Cruel Hill continues for ½ mile through the cool and shady forestry plantation, eventually levelling out and becoming a far less severe climb.

Just where the main forest track bears to the right to climb up to yet another Enmore road, follow the bridleway on the left that twists-and-turns up through the woodland to reach open farmland. Keeping the hedgerow to your right, continue on to a concrete reservoir from where there are fine views eastwards towards Glastonbury and the Mendips. Beyond this point, a bridleway continues down to a country lane, where you follow the path opposite through Rackhouse Copse and onto Broomfield Hill. This is common land, rough grazing pasture, where whortleberries and bracken abound.

Continue across the hilltop, taking the right-hand fork at the two junctions, until you arrive at a beech-lined path. The stile on the right a little way along this track is the start of a short detour should you wish to visit the *Traveller's Rest Inn*. It is actually worth following this path for a few yards to obtain an excellent view to the west that takes in the main Quantock Ridge, Hinkley Point Power-station and Bridgwater Bay. Your curiosity – or thirst – satisfied, continue along the beech-lined track to the Broomfield road, turn left and in less than one mile you will reach the village and Fyne Court.

Historical Notes

Fyne Court, whose origins date back to the early 17th century, was the ancestral home of the Crosse family. 'Was' is a wholly appropriate word to use, since a major fire in

1898 destroyed a large part of the site. What remains – a coach house, stables, the detached library, and a laboratory – is now the home of the Somerset Trust for Nature Conservation. The laboratory provides a clue to the identity of the most famous member of the Crosse family – Andrew (1784–1855) – a truly eccentric electrical scientist. During his lifetime, he lived at Fyne Court surrounded by a perfect chaos of apparatus. Even the family plate was not safe, as teapots, tankards and spoons were consigned to the crucible to produce chemically pure silver. Glasses and china were employed to produce batteries for experiments, and a luckless housemaid dusting items of brass might receive a shock that sent her flying across the room! Such was life at Fyne Court during Andrew Crosse's lifetime, when even the dinner-hour was a 'mere accident in the day's arrangements'. His two main areas of interest were studying the process of crystallisation as current was passed through various solutions, and recording electrical reactions obtained from over 1 mile of insulated wire strung around the trees at Broomfield. The scientifically-minded can read accounts of his work in the 1825 and 1854 proceedings of the British Association. His most renowned experiment occurred when he passed electricity through a new untried solution. An electrified stone produced whitish excrescences which later enlarged and assumed the form of a perfect insect. 'After a few days they detached themselves from the stone and moved about at pleasure'. To some people, this suggested that 'the electrician' had created life. Crosse never ventured a personal opinion on the experiment for the very good reason that he was 'never able to form one'.

Broomfield. The Somerset historian, Collinson, recorded the following thoughts in his volume 'The History of Somerset' –

> 'It is beautifully varied with swelling hills and deep romantick vales, and commanding a great variety of landscapes and very extensive prospects'.

For a writer noted for his sobriety, that is praise indeed! In the past, Broomfield was a much larger community. However, the agricultural slump of 1870–1914 that brought about rural depopulation across the nation did not leave Broomfield unscathed. Between 1831 and 1901, the population of the village fell from 503 people to 342. Today, it is less than 200. Where once there were five large family estates, today just the Herbert Tetton Estate remains. More than 40 houses have gone since the boom days of the village, and 1933 saw the closure of the village school. Whereas in 1914 it could boast 52 pupils, the few youngsters left in the village today are bussed to Kingston-St-Mary. The Church of St Mary and All Saints, however, still stands as the centre of village life. Of special note within the church are the richly carved bench-ends, perfect 16th century examples of traditional English craftsmanship. On the floor of the tower is a brass effigy to Richard Dulverton, unique insofar as it is the only example in Somerset of a priest in mass vestments. It is unfortunate that the head is missing! The inscription reads: 'Richard Dulverton 1443, chaplain, who governed this church in a praiseworthy manner, to the honour of God, the Blessed Mary, and All Saints for twenty-three years. He sumptuously repaired and magnificently decorated it'.

Ruborough Camp, high on Wind Down, is a Roman hill fort. It is unusually triangular in shape, and its outer earthworks are clearly defined to this day, albeit shrouded in the tangled undergrowth of the Forestry Commission's plantation. As you climb Cruel Hill, the north-facing ramparts lie on your left-hand side. Legends surround the Camp, including one story that beneath the ramparts lay an underground castle where vast treasures were hidden.

Jack Horner's 'Plum': Mells and the Eastern Mendips

Introduction: The casual visitor could be forgiven for thinking that the Mendips consist of the spectacular gorge at Cheddar, the impressive cavern at Wookey Hole and one-or-two moderately imposing hills thereabouts. In reality, the ancient Forest of Mendip stretched from the Black Rock in the Axe estuary near Weston eastwards to Cottle's Oak on the edge of Frome. East Mendip, the countryside between Wells and Frome, lies well away from the tourist trail. While the landscape may lack the spectacular natural features found further west, there is a much greater sense of human history and interest here. Mells, just a few miles west of Frome, is widely held to be among the most beautiful villages in Somerset. If the cottages with their 'holy grey-ness' were not enough, there is the magnificent Church of St Andrew, lying alongside the Tudor manor house of the Horner family. Naturally, local tradition links the manor with the 'plum' in 'Little Jack Horner', a tale described in the historical notes. If the manor is where the aristocrats ruled supreme, the valley of the Mells Stream was home to an altogether different family, the Fussells. These were industrialists, 19th century ironmasters, a complete contrast to the landed gentry up in the village. To escape from Mells and its ruling dynasties, the ramble takes us onto Barrow Hill, a fine viewpoint over this far-flung corner of north eastern Somerset.

Distance: A 5½-mile circuit with few real climbs to exercise those leg muscles. A pleasant half-day's excursion.

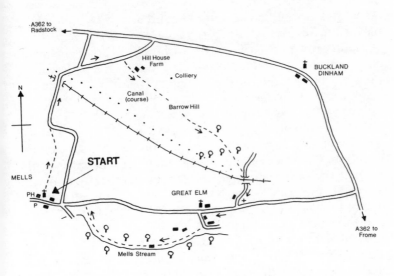

Refreshments: At the end of the walk, right in the centre of Mells, welcome sustenance can be obtained at the *Talbot Inn*.

How to get there: Mells lies just a couple of miles off the A362 Frome to Radstock road. A mile or so out of Frome, turn left onto the unclassified road signposted to Great Elm and Mells. In the centre of the village, there is room for careful parking on the road outside the *Talbot Inn*, alongside the fine medieval street that leads to St Andrew's Church. (GR 727492)

The Walk: The ramble begins at Mells Church. From here, search out the avenue of clipped yews on the northern side of the churchyard. At the end of this avenue, have fun negotiating a most ornate stile that leads into the fields beyond. Continue northwards across the first two fields, in both cases making for the gateway directly opposite. In the third field, aim for the far left-hand corner where a stone stile brings you onto the Mells to Buckland Dinham road.

91

As you cross the fields from the church, it is worth looking back towards Mells to see the fine 16th century manor.

Maintain a northerly course towards Buckland Dinham, climbing Conduit Hill as it crosses the Frome to Radstock railway. The muddy ditch immediately north of the line is what remains of the Dorset and Somerset Canal! At the hilltop, with its distant views southwards towards Gare Hill and Alfred's Tower, you reach a road junction. Turn right, along Collier's Lane, and in ½ mile follow the drive on the right-hand side that leads to Hill House Farm. Pass to the right of the farm buildings, and continue across Barrow Hill along an enclosed – and often muddy – footpath. In the valley to your left stands the solitary chimney of the long-disused Buckland Dinham Colliery. At one time, there were dozens of mines in the North Somerset countryside. Sadly, the last pit at Writhlington near Radstock closed in 1973. The enclosed path eventually ends and the right-of-way continues across the large field on the hilltop.

At the far side of this field, cross the stile and aim for the right-hand side of the copse ahead. All the while there are extensive views of the north-east Somerset countryside. Alongside the copse, cross the stile and follow the hedgerow beyond until it meets another enclosed path which is followed onto the lane that leads to Great Elm. Hidden in the trees to the south of the footpath across Barrow Hill are a number of depressions in the ground. These are the remains of a series of locks built to carry the Dorset and Somerset Canal up the hillside.

Turn right at the lane, turn right at the next road junction, and continue into Great Elm. In the village, take the first turning on the left that drops downhill towards the valley of the Mells Stream. This turning is almost directly opposite the village Church. In less than 200 yards, the road bears sharply to the left in front of a row of cottages. At this point, your path leaves the road as you turn to the right to follow a footpath down to the river. The next mile is truly delightful as the path borders the Mells Stream through a steep sided and thickly wooded valley.

Half a mile on, we pass the remains of the Fussell's iron works. It is worth hunting around between the footpath and the river to discover the many fascinating remnants of this industry – kilns, channels, old water-wheels, sluices and tramlines – a paradise for the industrial archaeologist! High on the hilltop to the left lies Tedbury Camp, whilst on the right-hand side is Wadbury Camp, both probably Iron Age in origin. The riverside path joins the Great Elm to Mells road, where you turn left to return to Mells and its magnificent Church and perhaps the nearby Talbot Inn for refreshment.

Historical Notes

Mells was originally just one small part of the far-flung empire of Glastonbury Abbey. New Street, with its medieval terraces leading to St Andrew's Church, is an arm of what was intended to be a cruciform street layout; 15th century town-planning! Designed by Abbot Selwood in 1470, it has been likened to a village counterpart of Vicar's Close in Wells. At the Dissolution, the estate passed into the hands of the Horner family. Local tradition maintains that the manor of Mells is none other than 'the plum' in the 'Little Jack Horner' nursery rhyme. The tale holds that Jack Horner was steward to Abbott Richard Whiting at the time of the Dissolution. Jack Horner was despatched to London with the deeds to a number of manors that were part of the rich demesne of the Abbey, all in an attempt to placate Henry VIII. Jack Horner held back one of the deeds for himself, which turned out to be none other than Mells manor!

There is perhaps little truth in this tale, although Thomas Horner did acquire the manor at about that time. The Horners operated a strict feudal regime in Mells, illustrated by the way in which the traditional Michaelmas Monday sheep fair in the village was stopped by the family. The Horner family objected to the bunch of ruffians who would disrupt the Sabbath each year preparing the fair!

St Andrew's Church, Mells, is built of limestone oolite and represents a perfect example of the Somerset Perpendicular Parish Church. Pevsner hesitates as to its age, with the scales falling in favour of the 15th or early 16th century. Certainly, he was impressed by the construction of the tower whose 'arrangement of buttresses and pinnacles is as ingenious as any in Somerset'.

Naturally, the influence of the Horner family dominates St Andrew's. The family vault is housed in the Horner Chapel, where the centre-piece is an equestrian statue of Edward Horner who fell in France in 1917. Crafted by Sir Alfred Munnings, it represents this distinguished painter's first venture into the field of sculpture. Raymond Asquith, son of the Liberal Prime Minister, married into the Horner family, which explains the richness and variety of the famous connections with Mells. Raymond Asquith's memorial on the south wall exhibits the handiwork of Sir Edwin Lutyens, the designer of the Cenotaph in Whitehall, who also designed the gravestones of Sir John and Lady Horner alongside the east wall of the churchyard. This corner of the burial ground reads like a page out of 'Who's Who', with Ronald Knox – the Roman Catholic Priest and Scholar, Siegfried Sassoon and Lady Violet Bonham-Carter all finding their earthly resting-place hereabouts. Personally, I prefer to recall an old weathered tombstone close-by that was reputed to carry the following inscription:

> 'All my inward friends uphorred me and they whom I loved are turned against me. My kinsfolk have failed me and my familiar friends have forgotten me. William Leecox husband of Rachell Leecox who departed April ye 16, 1700.'

Fussells were great ironmasters in this part of Somerset. In the valley of the Mells Stream, a complex site was established in 1744, ¼ mile long and containing canals, weirs, underground water-courses, and vast arches that housed water-wheels. There could hardly have been a more marked contrast than with the sophisticated Horners in the nearby manor, who unsurprisingly were engaged in frequent wrangles with the Fussells over their many industrial projects.

The Fussells took over a derelict ironworks and built their fortune upon scythes, axeheads, shovels, reaping hooks and all manner of edging tools. The works could not have had a more picturesque setting, deep in a heavily wooded narrow valley, although this was probably lost on the 250 men who worked here when Fussell's was at its peak. The Reverend John Skinner in his *Journal of a Somerset Rector* noted that:

> 'we confine people in bonds more heavy to be borne than any of the most cruel Indian planters ever imposed on their property'

after visiting Fussell's 'Iron Valley'. By 1857, James Fussell had wealth enough to repay some of his debt to the local community who toiled long and hard at the business of tool-making, which by now had spread to nearby Great Elm, Chantry, Railford and Nunney. A church and a school were built at Great Elm, the school being immortalised in Helen Mather's *Coming Thro' the Rye*. With the falling demand for edging tools, the Fussell's ironworks inevitably declined and, to quote a volume of local industrial archaeology, are now 'ruinous with simply a weir and complicated building pattern surviving'.

The Dorset and Somerset Canal was originally planned as a link between Bristol and Poole. Due to opposition from landowners, however, the proprietors had to be content with a route scheduled to run from the Kennet and Avon Canal at

Bradford-on-Avon to a point near Blandford Forum. There were also provisions for a branch westwards from Frome to the Somerset coalfield at Nettlebridge. The relevant Act, passed in 1796, stipulated that the Nettlebridge branch should be cut first.

Work on the branch commenced, but the construction of an aqueduct, several bridges and a tunnel cost £66,000, double the cash budget for this part of the canal. Funds were exhausted, further cash was not forthcoming, and the whole project was abandoned in 1803. On the main line of the canal, not one turf was cut. The ramble crosses Barrow Hill, site of some major engineering works on the Nettlebridge branch. A series of 'balance locks', invented by James Fussell the ironmaster, were planned to carry the canal down the hillside. A successful demonstration of a trial lock in 1800 (on a public right-of-way at GR. 735505) led to the start of work on five others further east. None was ever completed. The remains of these locks are a series of depressions across Barrow Hill, noted in the walk directions (GR 744503, but not on a right-of-way). Balance locks consisted of two chambers divided by a central wall, each containing a water-tight box into which a barge could be floated. By a system of wheels and chains, one box would rise as the other descended some 20 ft.